ROBERT M. GURNEY
ARCHITECT

ROBERT M. GURNEY
ARCHITECT

THE MASTER ARCHITECT SERIES

images
Publishing

Published in Australia in 2016 by
The Images Publishing Group Pty Ltd
ABN 89 059 734 431
6 Bastow Place, Mulgrave, Victoria 3170, Australia
Tel: +61 3 9561 5544 Fax: +61 3 9561 4860
books@imagespublishing.com
www.imagespublishing.com

Copyright © The Images Publishing Group Pty Ltd 2016
The Images Publishing Group Reference Number: 1104

All rights reserved. Apart from any fair dealing for the purposes of private study, research, criticism or review as permitted under the Copyright Act, no part of this publication may be reproduced, stored in a retrieval system or transmitted in any form by any means, electronic, mechanical, photocopying, recording or otherwise, without the written permission of the publisher.

Title:	Robert M. Gurney Architect: The Master Architect Series / Robert M. Gurney.
ISBN:	9781864705782 (hardback)
Series:	Master architect series.
Subjects:	Gurney, Robert M. Architecture, Modern—21st century. Architecture, Domestic—United States—21st century. Architecture—United States—Designs and plans. Architects—United States—Biography.
Dewey Number:	720.92
Production manager:	Rod Gilbert
Senior editor:	Gina Tsarouhas
Layout designer:	Jason Phillips
Assisting editor:	Bethany Patch

Printed on 157gsm GoldEast paper by Everbest Printing Investment Limited,
in Hong Kong/China

IMAGES has included on its website a page for special notices in relation to this and our other publications. Please visit www.imagespublishing.com.

CONTENTS

6 INTRODUCTION

SELECTED WORKS

12 4 SPRINGS LANE
24 308 MULBERRY STREET
38 APARTMENT 24
48 BECHERER HOUSE
60 BM MODULAR ONE
72 BRANDYWINE HOUSE
84 DIFFICULT RUN RESIDENCE
96 HAMPDEN LANE HOUSE
106 HOUSE ON SOLITUDE CREEK
118 KOMAI RESIDENCE
130 LORBER TARLER RESIDENCE
140 LUJAN HOUSE

152 LYON PARK HOUSE
164 MOHICAN HILLS HOUSE
178 NEVIS POOL AND GARDEN PAVILION
186 OVERLOOK ROAD HOUSE
200 RIGGINS HOUSE
214 SEA DEL HOUSE
228 SHARMA MATHUR HOUSE
240 TRED AVON RIVER HOUSE
256 TWINING ROAD HOUSE RENOVATION
270 WATERGATE APARTMENT
282 WISSIOMING2

296 CREDITS

INTRODUCTION

The vast majority of houses constructed today are anemic replications of beloved houses built in a bygone era. Synthetic reproductions of time-honored materials and thoughtless design process predominates. Wooded sites with rolling topography are leveled and rendered treeless. Molded styrene, plastics with embossed wood grain, and foam covered with resin reduce materials to flat, superficial images. Vinyl windows with artificial muntin bars are employed with no regard for orientation. This greatly compromises our sensual gratification and ecological awareness.

Once exposed to natural forces these houses will deteriorate rapidly and require great and unnecessary expense to repair or replace. Environmental illness and unfavorable response to synthetic materials, carcinogenic adhesives and suspect plastics will reinforce the notion that we respond to natural materials physically as well as psychologically. The projects that follow in this book are an attempt to reinforce a belief that architecture must break from unnatural and unhealthy imitation.

The 23 projects illustrated are located either within the Washington, DC metropolitan area, United States, or outside of Washington, DC, within a three-hour drive. This affords a unique opportunity to work on a variety of housing types, including urban, suburban and rural projects. Included are projects located in iconic Washington apartment buildings, such as the Watergate and 2101 Connecticut Avenue, as well as row dwellings located in the heart of Washington and houses constructed in the neighboring and outlying Maryland and Virginia suburbs. Buildings outside of the metropolitan area include a house near the Blue Ridge Mountains in Virginia, a house on farmland near Charlottesville, Virginia, and houses located on the Maryland eastern shore and coastal Delaware.

In addition to the diversity of locations, these projects vary in size. Projects range from a single-room pool pavilion and a one-bedroom apartment in the Watergate, to a renovation-addition project in Great Falls, Virginia, that includes comprehensive site reorganization and comprises over 14,000 square feet (1300 square meters) of new and renovated spaces. All of the projects are modern, ordered and meticulously detailed. The projects are site specific and filled with light, including the narrow row house projects that are inherently dark.

Whether working in complex historical districts or on vacant sites, the design process involves an understanding of site-specific issues of location, landscape, history, availability of materials and construction methods. For example, 308 Mulberry Street (page 24), constructed in the early 19th century, is centrally located in the historical district of Lewes, Delaware. Lewes is popularly known as an 18th century coastal town commemorated for being the site of the earliest European settlement in Delaware. In combination with a series of additions, this project involved extensive renovations to the historical fabric of the house. Painstaking research yielded significant information that fostered a complete restoration of the deteriorating building envelope. As another example, 4 Springs Lane (page 12), in rural Rappahannock County near the foothills of the Blue Ridge Mountains, is constructed on rock outcroppings and employs local stone in the construction. Tred Avon River House (page 240), in Easton, Maryland, is elevated on a concrete base to withstand expected, future flooding and high winds. An understanding of current technology, attention to detail, and awareness of location, landscape and history, lead to design solutions that respect historical, topographical and regional context, without being revivalist.

Materials are employed with honesty, integrity and ecological awareness. FSC (Forest Stewardship Council) certified wood siding is typically installed as a rainscreen providing ventilated wall systems that afford healthier interiors and reduce future maintenance. Regionally quarried stone lessens shipping costs while supporting local economies. Many of the projects employ energy efficient systems, incorporating geo-thermal wells, photovoltaic cells and evacuated tube solar collectors. Buildings are sited to optimize daylight and withstand negative environmental impacts where possible. Expanses of glass are insulated with low-emissivity coatings and filled with argon gas. When deep overhangs are not employed, solar sensors frequently activate concealed shades to reduce solar gain.

The work in this book is pragmatic. It is not theory based, there is no social agenda and there is not a singular design principle or manifesto. At the simplest level, the projects endeavor to organize spaces and meet a pre-established budget. Optimistically, the projects aspire to provide spaces that respond to unique site conditions, while manipulating light, color, texture, form and geometry. The culminating result is architecture that is simultaneously complex and distilled, providing interior spaces that are active and intricate, tranquil and minimal.

SELECTED WORKS

4 SPRINGS LANE

Rappahannock County, Virginia

Rolling topography, open fields and woodlands constitute the 24-acre (9.7-hectare) site in Rappahannock County, Virginia, where this new house is located. Extensive site investigation, including erecting scaffolding at various locations, resulted in the placement of the house high on one of the hills, overlooking a meadow at the base of woodlands. The house is organized as a series of volumes, arranged linearly, and positioned to optimize distant views of the Blue Ridge Mountains. The structure itself becomes a threshold and defines a more intimate, manicured outdoor environment between the house and the edge of the forest. The linear organization allows the majority of spaces to maintain mountain views while providing accessibility to a terrace with the swimming pool and the manicured area.

The two-story living/dining space has floor-to-ceiling glass at each end, providing a lens through which to view the mountains from the terrace.

The rigorous, refined and geometric forms of the building are designed in sharp contrast to the undulating, natural landscape. The contrast is intended to magnify the beauty of the site while allowing the house to provide a framework to view the landscape. These views become the orienting device. Simple volumes comprised of glass, wood, stone, and fiber cement panels are combined to render a more complex composition while garnering a serene unity.

Interior spaces are active and intricate, tranquil and minimal. With vistas in all directions, large expanses of glass allow the landscape views to provide the primary sensory experience.

A geothermal HVAC system, energy-efficient appliances, wall and ceiling infrastructure with maximum insulation, a rain-screen cladding system, extensive daylighting, and solar-sensor shades are employed with the expectation of reducing fossil-fuel consumption. Large operable windows and doors are placed to provide natural ventilation

This house is pragmatic and pristine. Proportion, texture, and light organize and animate the project. The composition is simultaneously complex and distilled. Most importantly, the house provides a framework to experience an inherently beautiful landscape.

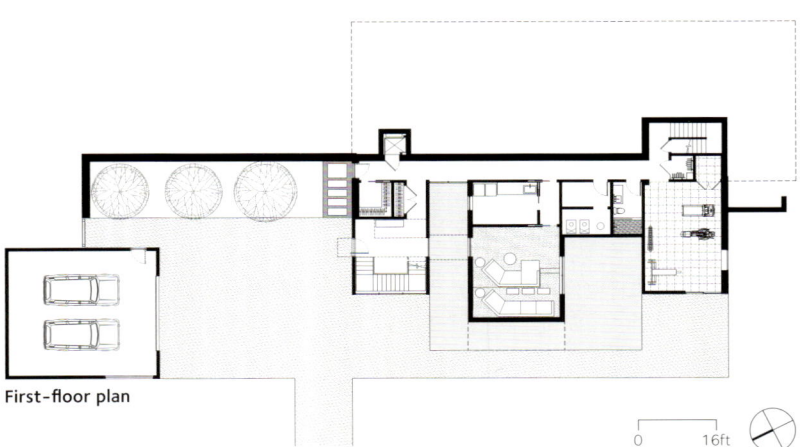

First-floor plan

0   16ft

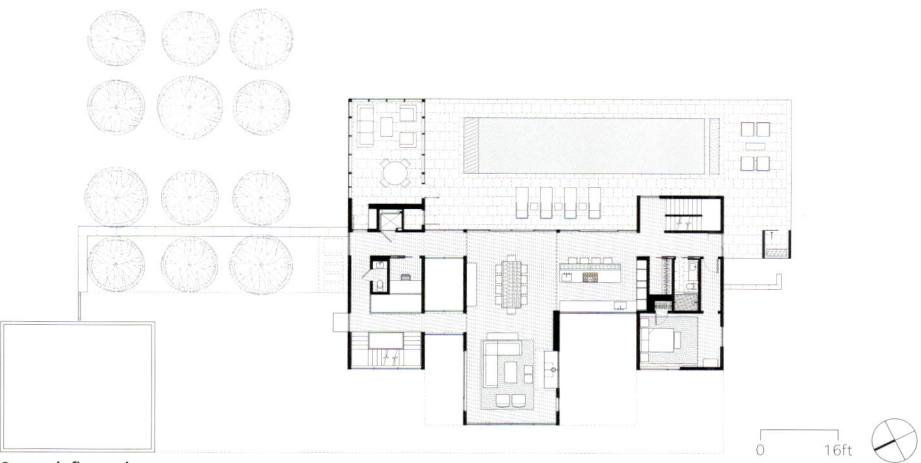
Second-floor plan

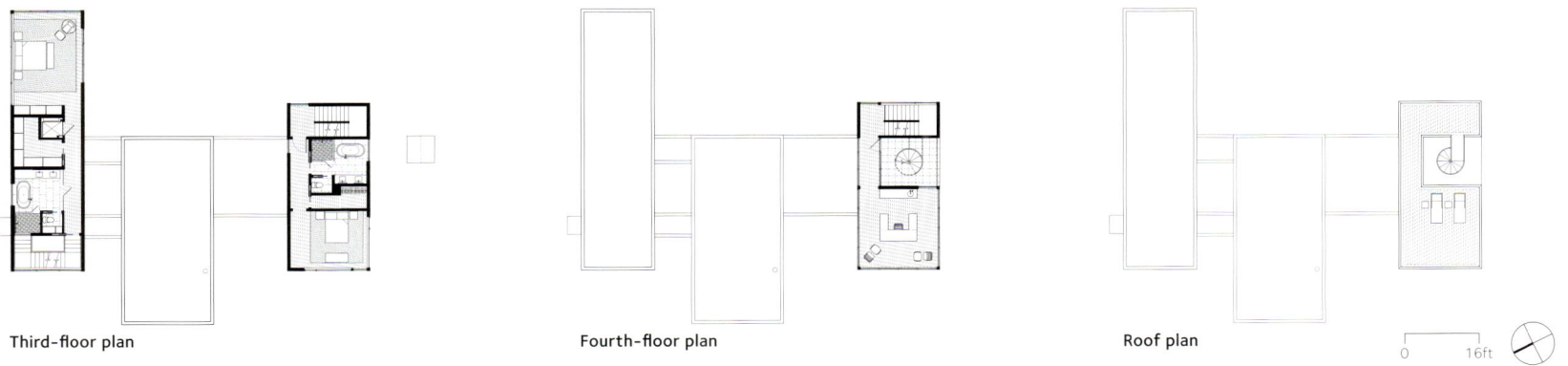

Third-floor plan   Fourth-floor plan   Roof plan   0   16ft

4 SPRINGS LANE   21

308 MULBERRY STREET

Lewes, Delaware

The small city of Lewes in Delaware, located on the eastern side of Sussex County, faces northeast into the mouth of the Delaware Bay. Lewes is popularly known as an 18th-century coastal town commemorated for being the site of the earliest European settlement in Delaware. Lewes is composed primarily of late-19th-century and early-20th-century building stock. The dominant building type is timber and the prevalent construction type is balloon framing. The starting point for this project is one such small house located at 308 Mulberry Street, originally constructed in the early 19th century in the heart of the historical district.

The current owner purchased the historical property in poor condition, with the intention of renovating the existing structure and adding a substantial extension and swimming pool. In the redesign, the exterior of the original structure has been meticulously restored. A shed-roofed screened porch, storage room, and poorly proportioned living space added to the back of the house in the early 20th century were removed.

The requested spatial requirements were substantial, and necessitated the footprint of the original building to be more than doubled. The design strategy was to allow the historical, two-story house to remain prominent in the overall composition. The requisite space would be accommodated in the original house and four additional structures that would engage the historical house in a minimally invasive fashion. The additions are conceived as one-story pavilions organized around a new swimming pool and large Deodar cedar tree, located at the rear of the property.

While the exterior of the original house is restored with historically correct detailing, the new pavilions are crisply detailed. Cedar shingled walls and roofs match the historical house, but without overhangs and trim. Large expanses of glass set in black steel frames punctuate the cedar walls. Tall red-brick chimneys and landscape walls add vertical and horizontal elements, completing the composition.

The original house now contains the main entry and four bedrooms. The interiors are decidedly modern with white walls void of trim, casings, moldings, and baseboard that engage white ash flooring. An open, floating staircase, glass walls, aluminum, and stainless steel contribute to the modern palette of elements and materials. In juxtaposition to the primarily white interiors of the original house, the interior of the new living pavilion is rich with a

variety of materials, including mahogany walls and ceilings, basalt flooring, white marble countertops and fireplace surround, and stainless-steel cabinetry. Walls of glass and a long skylight at the ridge allow light to flood the pavilion. Additional pavilions contain a bathroom, an exercise room and a screened porch. The screened porch, with Douglas-fir walls and ceilings, is located at the end of the swimming pool and contains a fireplace allowing the space to be used late into the fall.

This project is intended to embrace a small, historical house, to restore it, and allow it to contribute to the fabric of historical Lewes for many years to come. The project also attempts to provide generously proportioned, modern, light-filled spaces that coexist comfortably within the historical fabric.

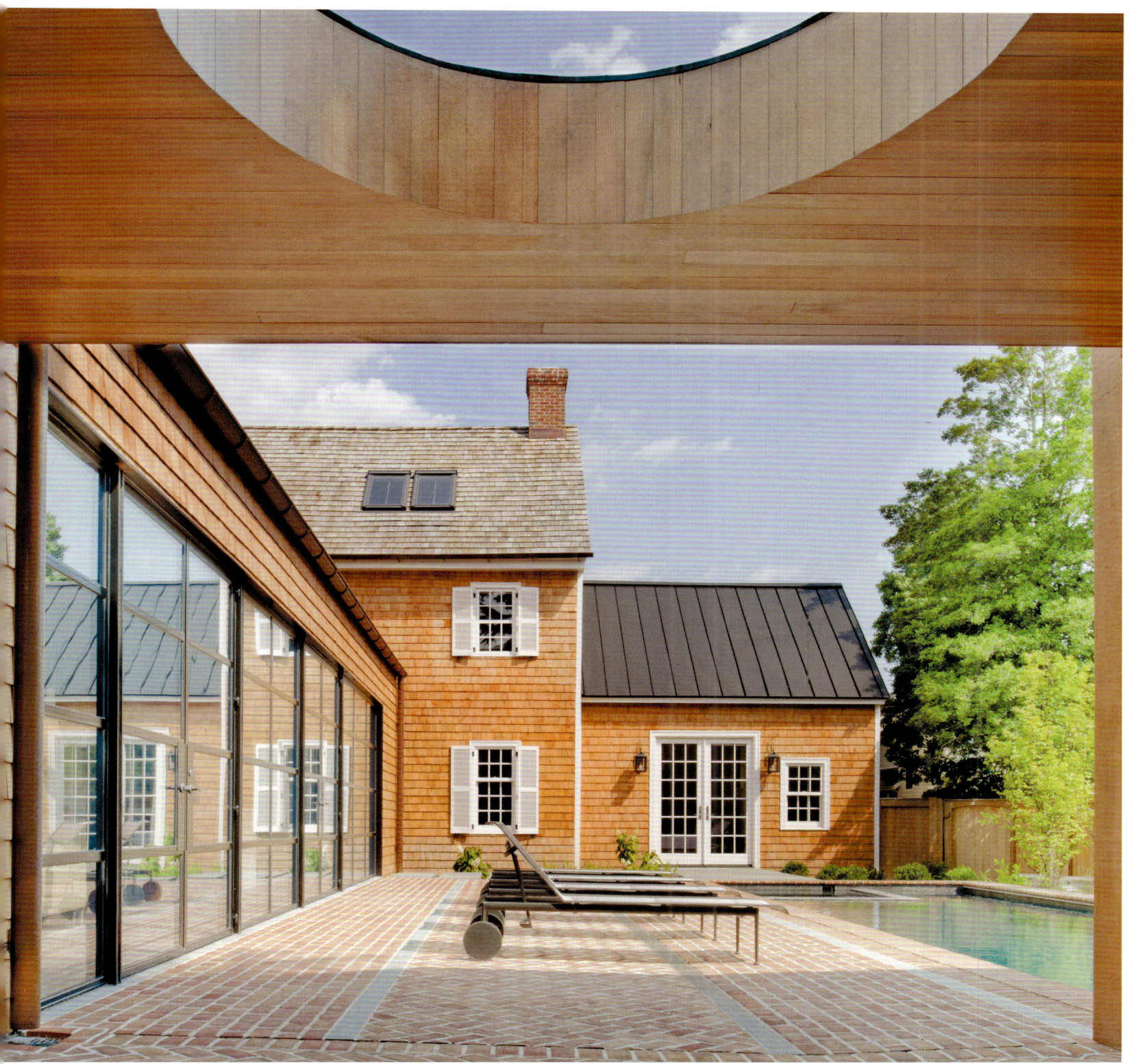

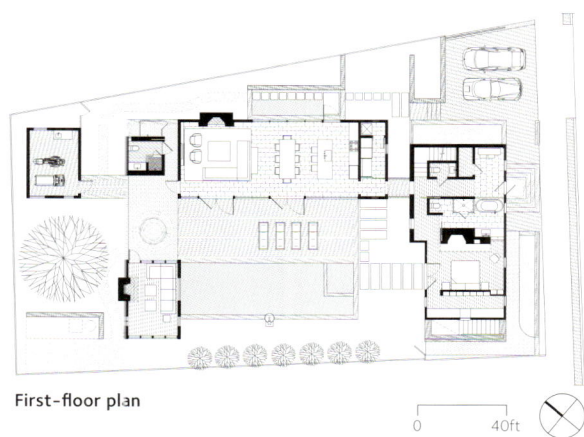

First-floor plan

0 40ft

308 MULBERRY STREET

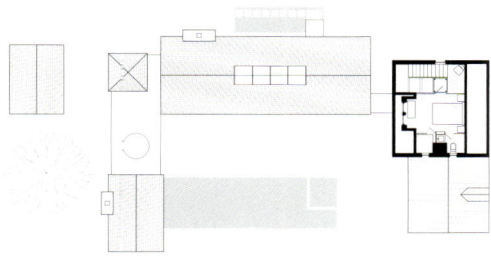

Third-floor plan

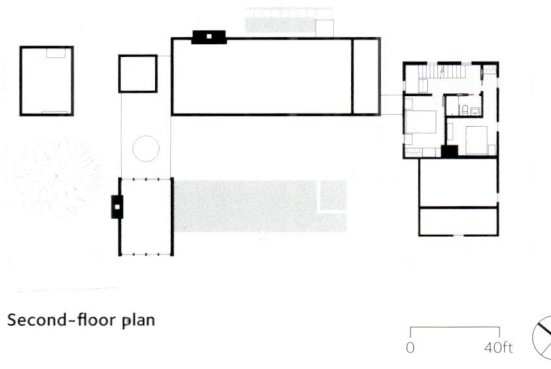

Second-floor plan

0　　40ft

APARTMENT 24

Washington, D.C.

The building at 2101 Connecticut Avenue, NW is located in the Kalorama neighborhood of Washington, D.C. and was built in 1928. This Spanish Colonial–style apartment building is designated as a contributing property to the Kalorama Triangle Historic District and is listed on the National Register of Historic Places. Interior spaces, including the main lobby and hallways, are ornate and elaborately detailed. The individual apartments are spacious, with ample windows and varying solar exposure; however, the units are compartmentalized, greatly reducing the sense of space.

Apartment 24 is a transformation of this traditional apartment typology. The design process was one of reduction, with the goal of creating a series of open, interconnected spaces filled with light. The interior was gutted and reorganized within a framework of existing concrete columns and beams, as well as electrical, plumbing and mechanical infrastructure. A centrally located line of columns and beams articulates the entry and main circulation gallery while modulating and articulating a hierarchy of spaces.

In the new scheme, the apartment is rigorously ordered and organized. A vista from the entry extends through the entire apartment, extending the sense of space. The kitchen, living and dining spaces are relocated to ensure that those spaces will receive the majority of sunlight, while the bedrooms and other secondary spaces are positioned toward the interior of the building.

The material palette, which includes dark-stained oak flooring, white oak cabinetry and paneling, zebrawood, glass, and aluminum, is intended to provide spatial unity and consistency throughout.

Cabinetry and millwork are deployed in a system of horizontal and vertical layers, and work to simultaneously define and unify spaces. Translucent glass panels, employed throughout the apartment, provide a sublime quality while allowing a subtle awareness of space beyond. Detailing throughout is crisp and minimal, contributing to an intended juxtaposition between Apartment 24 and the existing ornate interiors experienced prior to entering the new space.

This reorganization of spaces and open floor plan infuses a design that is intended to be more sensitive to modern lifestyles while demonstrating how a landmark, historical building continues to be a viable option for urban housing in Washington, D.C.

Floor plan

APARTMENT 24

APARTMENT 24

APARTMENT 24

BECHERER HOUSE

Earlysville, Virginia

Rolling pastures, bordered with dark, stained fences interspersed in woodlands, define the Albemarle County, Virginia, countryside, where this project is located. The new house is sited at the edge of woodland and on the crest of a hill, providing vantage viewpoints of the pastures and distant treetops.

The house is conceived as three gable-roofed pavilions that provide a threshold between the woodlands and the pastures, taking advantage of two very different scenic panoramas. The one-room-deep, central living pavilion contains large expanses of glass along two walls, affording views of both the woods and horse pastures. This configuration ensures that the space will be flooded with light at all times of the day throughout the year. A screened porch and bluestone terrace, running the length of the house, provides a stage to view sunsets over the pastures, while a manicured lawn and dry-stacked slate wall provides an ordered transition from the house to the woods beyond.

Gable roofs with black standing seam metal, clapboard siding, and the small scale of the separated pavilions evoke a familiar and comfortable rural vernacular, while the large expanses of glass, cement-board paneling, and crisp, minimal detailing render the house decidedly modern.

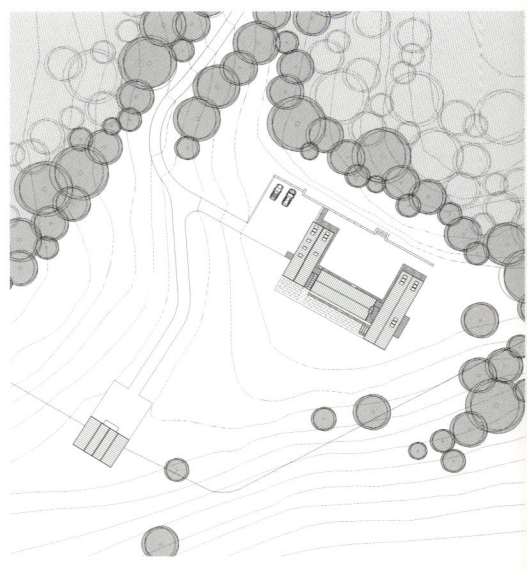

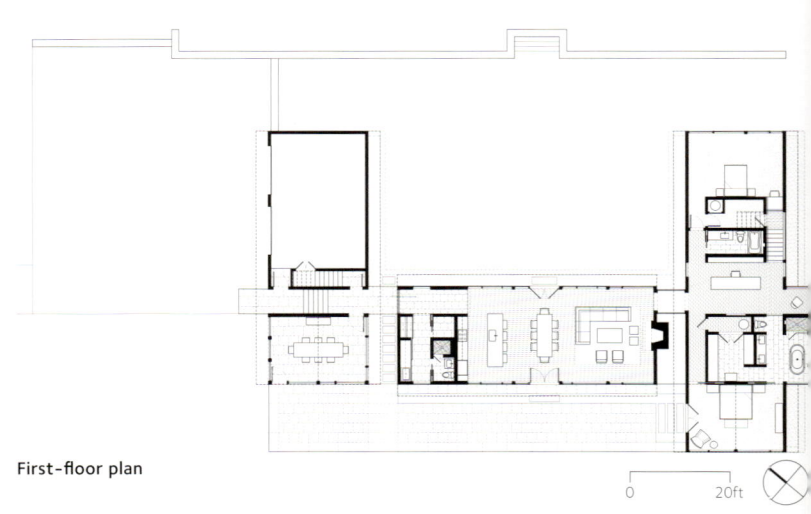

First-floor plan

BECHERER HOUSE 57

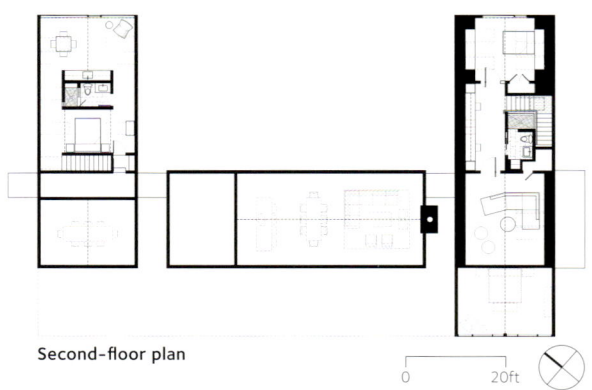

Second-floor plan

0 20ft

58

BM MODULAR ONE

Bethesda, Maryland

A successful builder/developer with a history of constructing modular houses purchased a lot in a desirable neighborhood near Washington, D.C. with the intention of building a spec house. When a potential buyer expressed interest in the lot, the developer proposed a modular house as a solution to a tight budget and time constraints. However, the Craftsman and Colonial-style modular houses typically built by the developer did not appeal to the potential client, who desired a light-filled, modern house.

The house is designed to both fulfill the wishes of the clients and to provide the developer with a 'modern house' typology that fills a void on their menu of modular houses. Relative to similarly sized custom houses in the expensive Washington, D.C. real-estate market, this house is designed to be flexible, efficient, and affordable.

bm Modular One is composed of 13 modules and was constructed in two weeks in a plant in southern Virginia. It was then shipped to the site on flat-beds and assembled on-site within two days. Energy-efficient shells arrived at the site with windows, plumbing, and electrical and HVAC ducting in place. The interiors were dry-walled and primed, ready for finishes. The foundation and basement were constructed with polished concrete floors on-site, while the modules were fabricated off-site. High energy-efficient goals are further enhanced as a result of a geothermal HVAC system, and tight, super-insulated exterior floor, wall, and roof systems.

The house employs repeatable parts that can be combined into custom configurations. This is exemplified by the fact that the modules are arranged to meet restrictive zoning requirements on an irregularly shaped lot. The modules are delivered primed, yielding a blank canvas, and allow for the extent and level of finishes to remain flexible. In this case, finishes include maple flooring, walnut millwork, aluminum stairs, and other materials specific to this client's preferences, while large expanses of glass are designed to allow for varying orientations. The house brings together durable corrugated-metal siding with stucco and Spanish cedar. The massing provides opportunities to combine several exterior materials so that the house can be adapted for different environments.

The first of an undetermined number of future versions, this house can be modified to meet differing clients' needs and fit varying sites. Modern and filled with light, the house employs all of the intended benefits of modular building without compromising proportion, light, scale, or texture.

BM MODULAR ONE 63

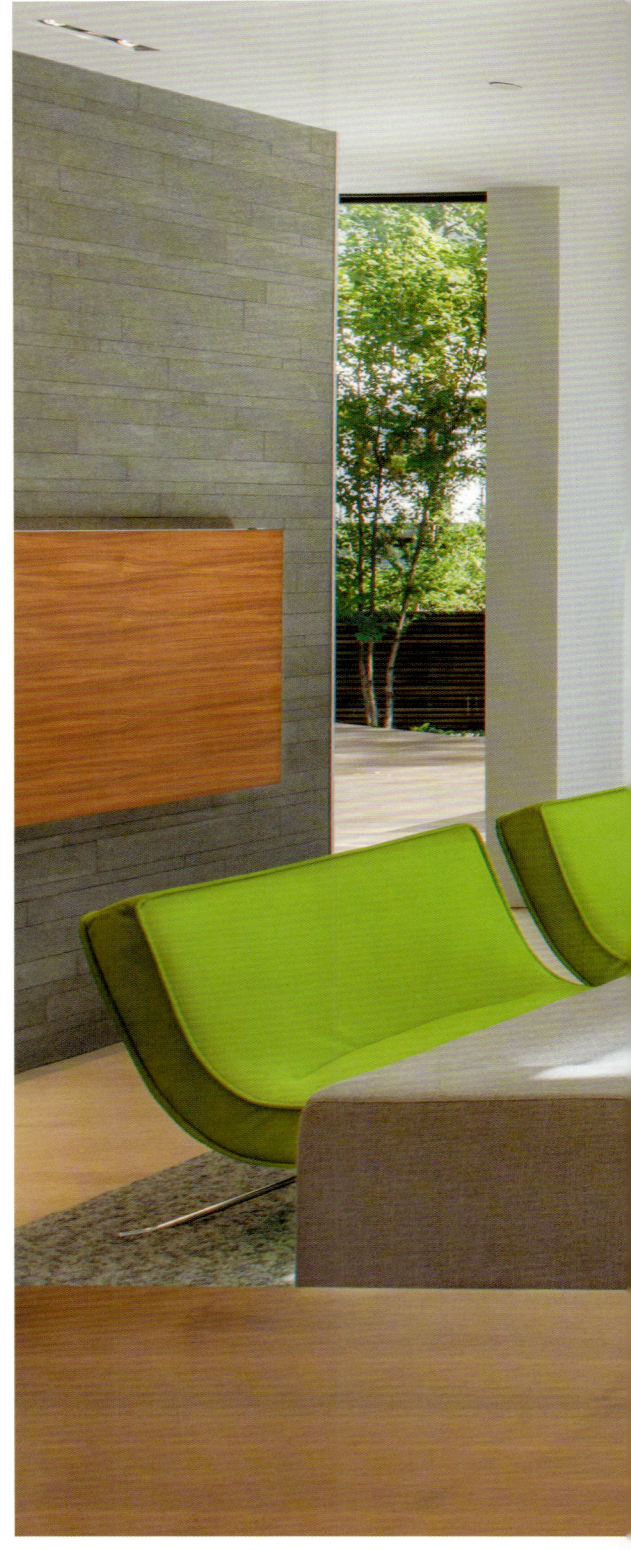

North–east elevation

South–west elevation

Third-floor plan

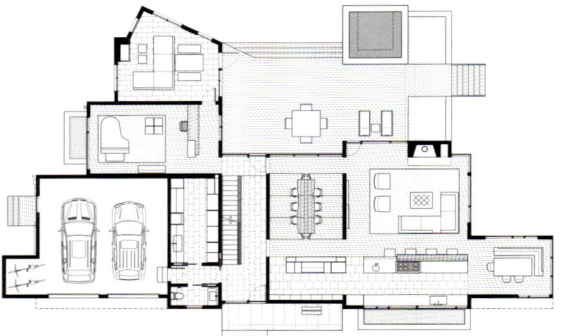
Second-floor plan

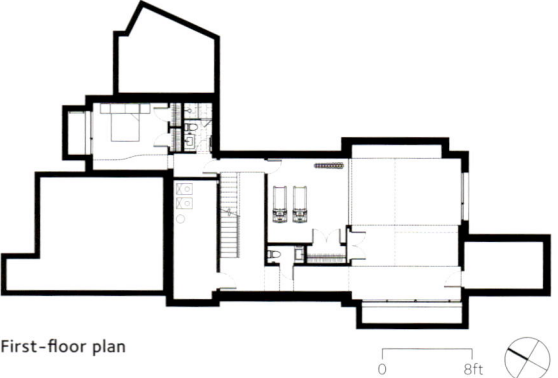
First-floor plan

0   8ft

BRANDYWINE HOUSE

Washington, D.C.

Located within close proximity to Rock Creek Park, and with easy access to the shops and restaurants on Connecticut Avenue, this large lot in northwest Washington, D.C. presented a desirable opportunity for a young family to build a new house in this sought-after neighborhood.

Designed to respect both the scale of neighboring houses and the rhythm of the streetscape, the project aligns with adjacent houses while retaining the vast majority of mature trees and green space located between the street and the house. Materials composing the exterior, which include stone, wood, and stucco, evoke traditional materials found throughout the neighborhood. The house appears relatively solid when viewed from the street, with strategically placed windows ensuring privacy to the street-facing spaces.

The 'L'-shaped house is organized around the outdoor living spaces and swimming pool, and is oriented towards the large, south-facing backyard. Floor-to-ceiling expanses of glass provide ample visual and physical connectivity to the terraces, the swimming pool, and the wooded landscape beyond. A screened porch, covered deck, rooftop deck, and balconies continue this dialogue. A small bridge and a stone path engage the house and terraces with the wooded, less manicured landscape at the rear of the property.

The interiors are warm, filled with light, and ordered with a clear spatial organization. Various wood species, including white oak, Santos mahogany, rosewood, and various zebrawoods (all forest-certified or reconstituted products), combine with limestone and various granites to provide a rich material palette. Generous use of skylights creates changing light conditions that activate the interior.

Despite the relatively large size of this house and the extensive use of glass, the house remains incredibly energy efficient. While the large numbers of windows and skylights provide generous daytime lighting, computer-programmed shading devices modulate solar gain. A geothermal HVAC system, including hydronic heating, combines with solar hot-water tubes and photovoltaic panels, aiming to provide a net zero-energy house.

This project is intended to be respectful of its established neighborhood while infusing a modern sensibility for aesthetics, functionality, ecology, and technology.

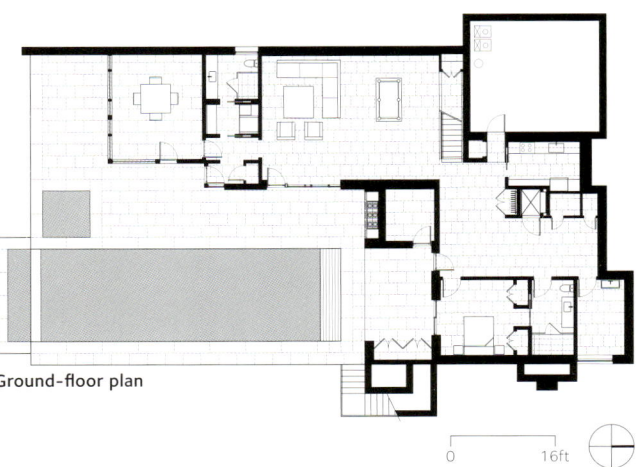
Ground-floor plan

BRANDYWINE HOUSE

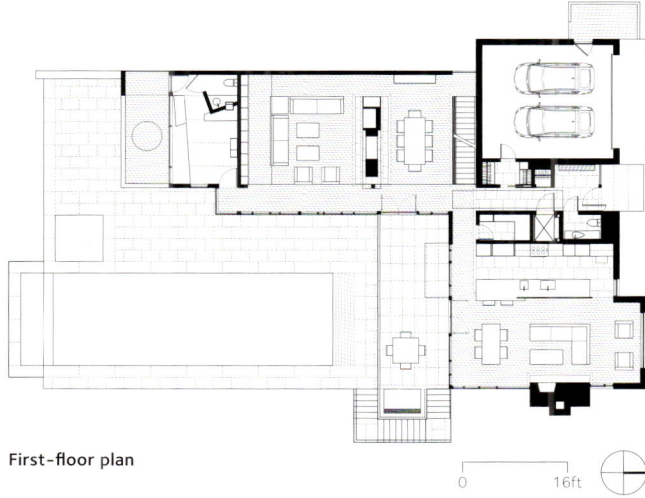

First-floor plan

BRANDYWINE HOUSE

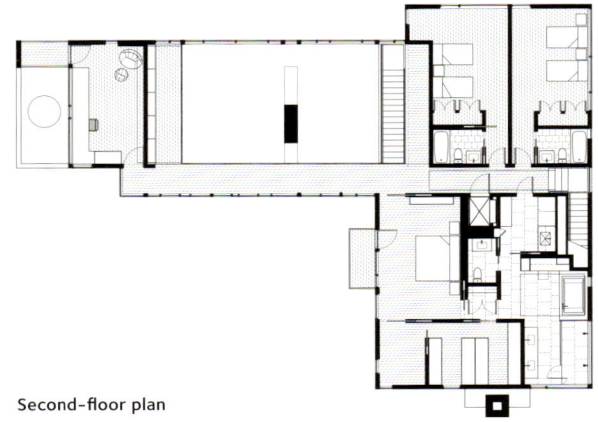
Second-floor plan

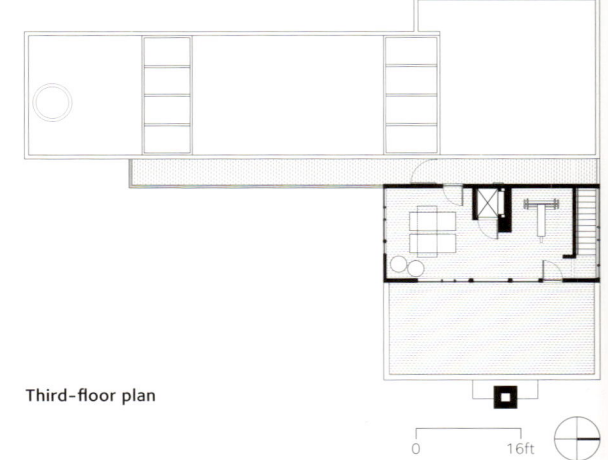
Third-floor plan

0　　16ft

BRANDYWINE HOUSE 81

BRANDYWINE HOUSE

DIFFICULT RUN RESIDENCE

McLean, Virginia

Located in McLean, Virginia, this project is sited on a 7-acre (2.8-hectare), steeply sloping, and wooded lot bordering a stream and parkland trail, known as Difficult Run. The scope of work involved a complete renovation of an existing house, a substantial addition to the house, a new detached garage and guest house, and a comprehensive reorganization of the site.

The pre-existing approach to the house involved a narrow, meandering driveway with limited parking space. Adjacent vegetation was overgrown, and in many places severely reduced the amount of light entering the house. As part of the renovation, extensive on-site parking was added to accommodate large family and corporate gatherings. A limestone wall with a custom-designed steel gate creates a threshold to the property. The new parking area and tree-lined approach to the house are delineated with a series of limestone and stacked slate walls arranged on an axis to the house and rendered with differing paving materials. A new garage and guesthouse structure is located to further define the parking area, and is organized around a large, mature Deodar cedar tree. A stone wall with a water element is introduced opposite the main entry and extends this principal axis. Stone paths and stairways, corten steel walls, gabion stone walls, a swimming pool with an infinity edge, a reflecting pool, terraces and decks, and structured plantings continue to organize the site and provide an abundance of outdoor living spaces.

The existing main structure, built in 1965, contained a series of interior and exterior spaces below a single, low-pitched roof with a ridgeline spanning diagonally above the orthogonally arranged spaces. An attached hexagonal volume contained the bedrooms. The space was wrapped in a muted palette of materials, including dark flagstone flooring, gray stone walls and fireplaces, and dark-wood walls and ceilings. This rendered existing interior spaces compartmentalized and dark, despite expanses of glass. In renovating the main house, all interior finishes were stripped, walls were removed, spaces were opened up, and windows were enlarged and replaced, in an effort to reflect the light rather than absorb it. A series of small additions were implemented as required, and located within the footprint of the existing roof. While the roof structure was retained, the ballast roofing was replaced with standing seam, terne-coated stainless steel. In addition, the board and batten siding was supplanted with a combination of dry-stacked slate, stucco, and limestone. The new window system comprises a custom steel curtain wall and steel windows with thin profiles. Interior finishes include Cambrian Cream stone and

dark-stained oak flooring; smoked oak, wenge, walnut, and lacquered millwork; glass; and honed, polished, and hammered absolute black granite. Detailing is crisp and minimal with no trim, casing, or baseboards.

The new addition encompasses a large library, five bedrooms and bathrooms, an exercise room, media room, laundry room, and other support spaces. These new spaces are stacked vertically but descend rather than ascend, minimizing the apparent size of the new structure as perceived upon entering the property, and working within the steeply sloping topography. The rooftop of the addition extends the slightly sloping roofline of the existing house, and folds up at the southern corner to capture light and to provide expansive views into the wooded landscape and stream below. Finishes and detailing continue the palette prescribed in the main house.

The new garage accommodates three cars, and the guesthouse includes two bedrooms. The massing and materials employed continue the language introduced in the main house.

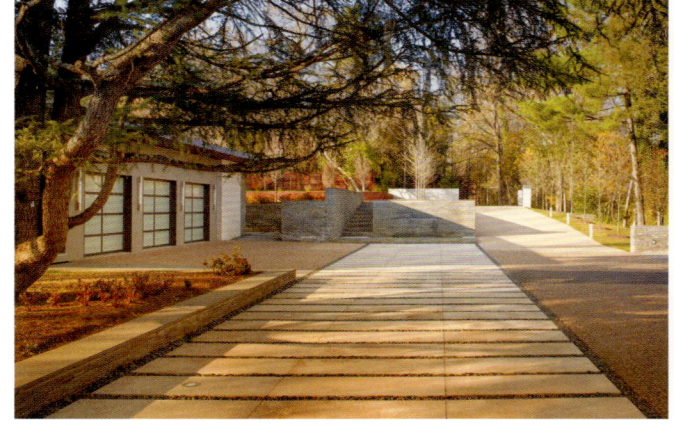

This is a large and comprehensive project that entails a total integration of site-specific requirements, landscape components, a complete renovation of a substantial structure, a significant addition, and a separate garage and guesthouse. The goal of this project was to incorporate all of these requirements in a cohesive, site-responsive manner that provides integrated interior and exterior spaces sensitive to the land the project occupies.

DIFFICULT RUN RESIDENCE

Basement plan

Lower-basement plan

0　　　40ft

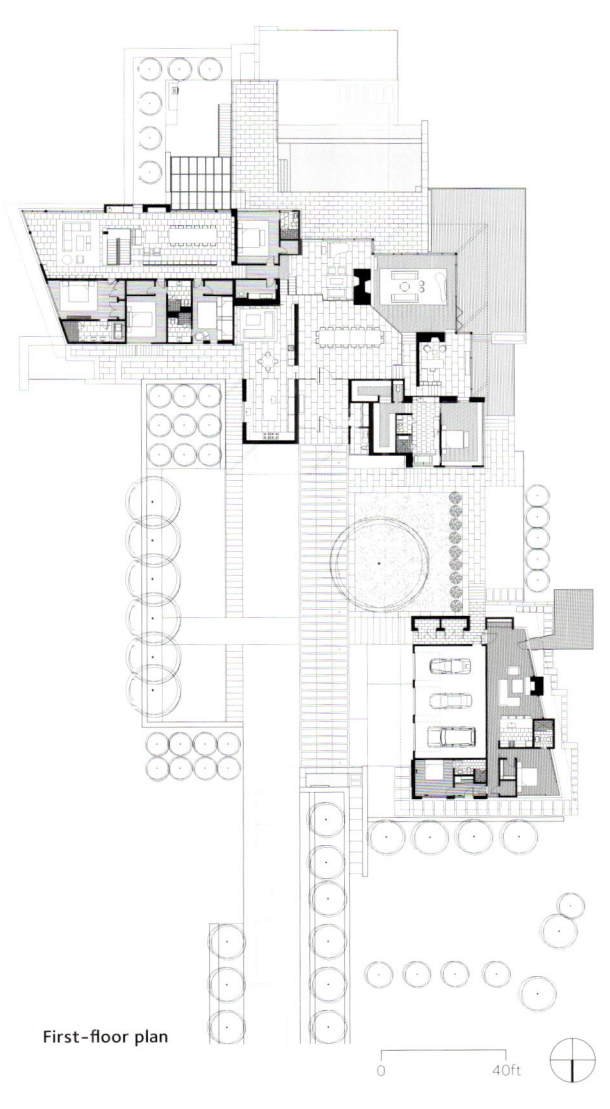

First-floor plan

0   40ft

DIFFICULT RUN RESIDENCE

DIFFICULT RUN RESIDENCE

HAMPDEN LANE HOUSE

Bethesda, Maryland

Edgemoore is an affluent neighborhood in Bethesda, Maryland, a suburb bordering northwest Washington, D.C. Mature trees and gardens line the streets of this neighborhood, within walking distance of downtown Bethesda.

Too often lately, many of the perfectly scaled houses inhabiting this neighborhood are being torn down and replaced with Craftsman-style houses on steroids, and pseudo-colonials far too large for their lots. Most of these new houses are built to the maximum size allowed by the zoning ordinances, with little regard for the scale of adjacent structures. Sites are rendered treeless, leaving little or no green space. These houses seem egregious, insensitive, and irresponsible.

The client for this project was a young, forward-thinking entrepreneur with no desire for a nostalgic or Revivalist-style house. He desired a house that was efficient with a minimal footprint, leaving the majority of the lot unoccupied by building and hardscape. The close proximity to urban downtown Bethesda warranted a house designed with closer ties to an urban area, rather than to the rural countryside that once informed the design of houses in Edgemoore.

After much deliberation, it was decided to remove an existing, inefficient structure, and replace it with a new one. The new house occupies an area one-third smaller than the area occupied by the original structure, and is sited to maximize green area on the property. Designed as a cube, the new house is approximately 2200 square feet (204.5 square meters) with no unused or underutilized spaces. The flat roof provides an additional 1100 square feet (102 square meters) of outdoor living space with views of treetops and the downtown Bethesda skyline.

Fenestration, composed of rectangular and square openings of various sizes, is arranged to optimize views to the green spaces while minimizing views of adjacent houses. A series of landscape walls orchestrate the relationship between the street, required parking court, and house. Interior spaces are open and light-filled, with crisp detailing. Walnut flooring provides a rich base for white walls and millwork, designed to be in juxtaposition with the charcoal-gray exterior walls.

This house represents a deliberate departure in both the thought process and the realization of current building trends in the neighborhood. Instead of building a large house with pretentious ties to the rural past, this new house is smaller with a stronger relationship to the modern, urban area that Bethesda has become. The house is intended to be more site-sensitive and environmentally conscious, and to provide comfortable, efficient living spaces.

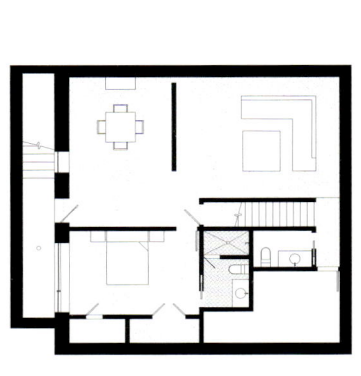

Basement-floor plan

First-floor plan

Second-floor plan

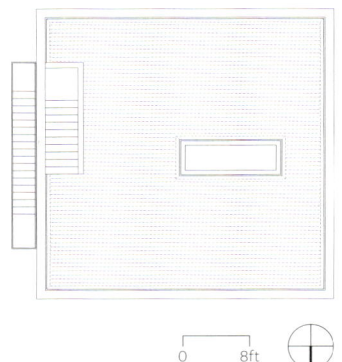

Roof plan

HAMPDEN LANE HOUSE

HOUSE ON SOLITUDE CREEK

St. Michaels, Maryland

The design of this house in St. Michaels, Maryland, was greatly influenced by environmental regulations, zoning requirements and restrictive building codes specific to this site. The existing Dutch Colonial–style house, built in 1989, was located within a 100-foot (30.5-meter) buffer zone on Solitude Creek, a small estuary in this Maryland Eastern Shore town. A recently adopted floodplain management ordinance mandated that no new structures be built within the buffer zone, and that all renovated or altered existing structures be updated to meet new zoning, building and environmental code requirements.

The existing house largely failed to take advantage of water views, the layout was not optimal, and as constructed, did not work programmatically for the new owners of this property. The existing structure was in poor condition, with rotted framing members and mold and mildew infiltration from previous floods. The house did not meet many of the new code requirements; most notably the requirement that any habitable structure be located above the newly designated base flood elevation. To maintain the proximity to the water, and to avoid building a new house *outside* the buffer zone (which would be a much greater distance from the shoreline), it was decided to remove the existing structure to the foundation, increase the height of the foundation 2 feet (61 centimeters), and build a new structure above this that would meet all of the new codes, ordinances, and regulations. Per these regulations, the footprint was not expanded or altered. While the new house is built above the existing foundation, a new covered entry porch is cantilevered beyond the foundation, permitted as long as the cantilevered section was not larger than the pre-existing stoop. A series of small decks and ramps extend to the landscape and are constructed to break apart in the event of a major storm or flooding.

The goals of the project were to take advantage of water views and provide light-filled spaces, while accommodating the owners' collection of modern art, which includes works by one owner, who is an artist specializing in abstract paintings. In response to a relatively tight budget, the buildings' massing and materials are simple and straight-forward. A combination of windows varying in size, shape and location animate the spaces, while providing controlled views of the water, pine forest and adjacent marshes.

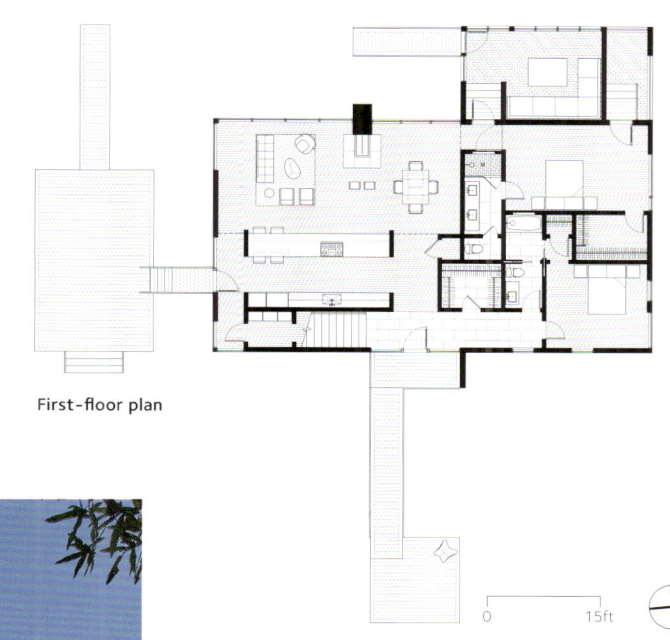

First-floor plan

0　15ft

HOUSE ON SOLITUDE CREEK

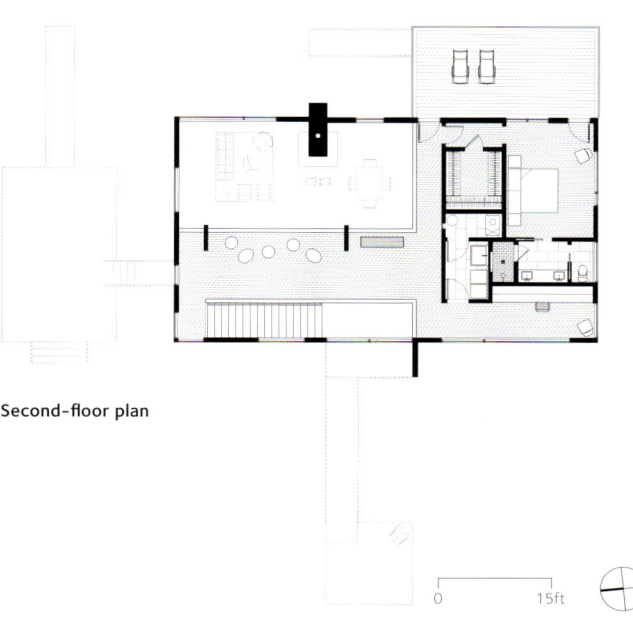

Second-floor plan

0 15ft

HOUSE ON SOLITUDE CREEK

HOUSE ON SOLITUDE CREEK

HOUSE ON SOLITUDE CREEK

KOMAI RESIDENCE

Alexandria, Virginia

A small, triangular corner lot in the Del Ray neighborhood of Alexandria, Virginia, was considered too small to accommodate a new house. For years, this lot mostly served the neighborhood as a dog-walking park. Zoning setbacks, and a height limit consistent with the adjacent, primarily one-story bungalows, Craftsman-style houses, and small colonials, reduced the buildable footprint and building envelope significantly. In addition, two off-street parking spaces were required. Developers struggled to provide a house that was both similar in style to neighboring houses and would fit onto the lot.

Two creative graphic designers who lived in the neighborhood viewed the lot with its inherent challenges as an opportunity to build a small, modern house that would allow them to downsize and remain in the neighborhood they loved. They purchased the lot, knowing their house would be site-responsive, but unlike the neighboring houses.

The program for the new house was relatively modest: an open living, dining and kitchen space, a first-floor master bedroom suite, a workspace, and a guest bedroom suite. In the design, the zoning setbacks largely informed the volume and massing. The house is constructed to the zoning setbacks on facing streets, which align with adjacent houses along the lengths of both blocks. While the house is two-stories tall and built to the maximum height limit, it is consistent with the average height of the 13 houses within the triangular block.

The house is organized around a double-height space containing the dining and living area. A bridge connects the second-floor office with the guest bedroom suite, and helps define the dining area. Three large skylights further animate the space, and in combination with large expanses of glass and Kalwall panels, the space is flooded with light. Finishes are kept minimal and the detailing is crisp. Spatial composition and natural light become the primary design tools.

Despite employing an architectural language dissimilar to its neighboring predecessors, the scale and height of this new house are consistent with them, and allow the house to integrate comfortably within this eclectic neighborhood.

Second-floor plan

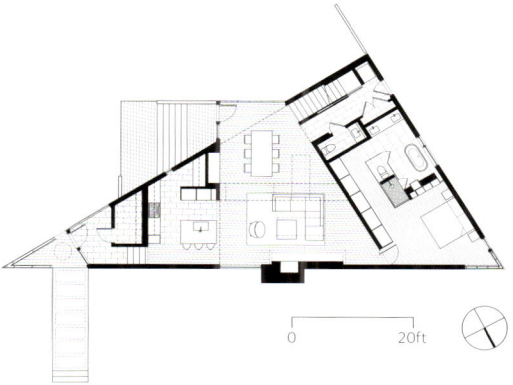

First-floor plan

KOMAI RESIDENCE

LORBER TARLER RESIDENCE
Washington, D.C.

Located in the Mount Vernon Square neighborhood of Washington D.C., an existing row house has been reimagined as a modern, light-filled urban dwelling for a professional couple. The compartmentalized interior of the existing house was gutted, and the rear façade and porch were removed. Surrounded by buildings on three sides, and limited to the existing 17-foot-wide by 30-foot-deep (5.2-meter-wide by 9.1-meter-deep) footprint, the new floor layout and open plan are intended to provide dynamic interior spaces in sharp contrast to the originally dark, cramped house.

Manipulation of natural light into this residence is a major component affecting the design of the project. A new stair and glass bridge system connects all three floors, with a skylight along the entire length and width of the new stair opening. The new rear façade is almost fully glazed, maximizing the amount of light obtainable from the eastern exposure. Inside, translucent panels between rooms offer further sources for natural light.

The stairwell is designed as a vertical core that organizes the project. While the open-riser staircases with glass rails and bridges provide transparency, a three-story, wood-paneled wall slices through the stairwell, integrating and defining adjacent spaces. This wall terminates inside the skylight well, allowing light from the skylight into the third-floor bedroom.

A ground-level terrace visually enlarges the living room and offers a private outdoor living space within the city. The terrace becomes an outdoor room with walls of glass, cement board, and mahogany. A galvanized-steel planter with bamboo and black river stone runs the length of the terrace, offering an opportunity for greenery in the urban setting.

This project relies on the verticality of the row-house typology to provide spacious volume, as opposed to a large floor area. Highly considered, well-crafted materials, and close attention to detail further enhance the spatial qualities of this project. A palette consisting of blue Venetian plaster, white terrazzo flooring, clear and dark stained rift-sawn white oak, aluminum, stainless steel, clear and translucent glass, painted steel, limestone, and granite are forged to enrich the spaces.

This house was built near the turn of the century, and is located in a historical district. The result of this renovation represents the coexistence of a modern vocabulary adapted to current living patterns within an existing, historically significant framework.

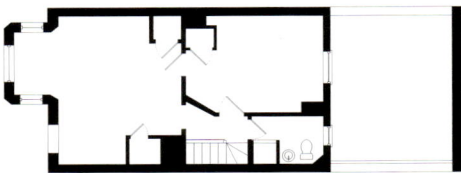
Upper-level floor plan (before)

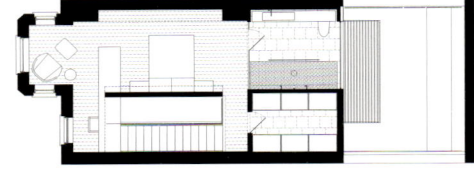
Upper-level floor plan (after)

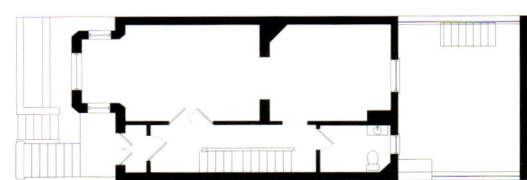
Entry-level floor plan (before)

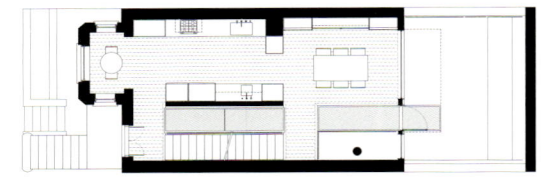
Entry-level floor plan (after)

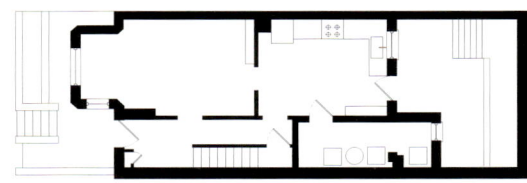
Lower-level floor plan (before)

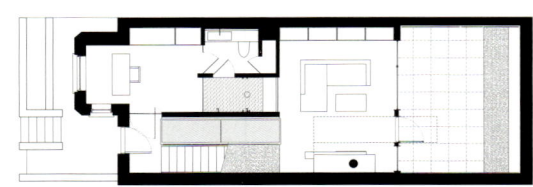
Lower-level floor plan (after)

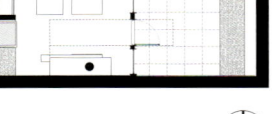

LORBER TARLER RESIDENCE

LUJAN HOUSE

Ocean View, Delaware

The Quillen's Point neighborhood, adjacent to the Chesapeake Bay in Ocean View, Delaware, is composed of modest houses on small lots. An eclectic mix of houses, gravel roads ending at the bay, and wooded lots provide a nostalgic, informal setting for this new house. The project site is near the end of Burbage Lane, the second lot from the bay. It is expected that the adjacent waterfront lot will eventually be developed.

In an effort to integrate living spaces with the outdoors, while maintaining privacy from Burbage Lane and neighboring houses, the scheme is organized around a centrally located garden. With 16-foot-high (4.9-meter-high) ceilings, the eastern volume contains the public living spaces. Continuous clerestory windows provide an abundance of natural light, allowing views to the treetops and sky, rather than to the adjacent houses. A 20-foot-wide (6-meter-wide) glass wall slides into a pocket, enhancing the relationship to the outdoors, and provides a sense of living in a garden. The two-story western volume comprises bedrooms and a small second-floor living space. A one-story glass link connects the eastern and western volumes, and visually opens to the central garden.

The house was conceived as two simple, flat-roofed volumes, varying in height, intersecting and overlapping a one-story circulation space that connects the volumes. The eastern volume is constructed with cement board, the western volume with corrugated siding, and the one-story connecting space with the ground-face concrete block. The exterior material palette is quiet and subdued. Materials are selected for their expected long-term durability, ease of installation, and cost. The impact of the one-story, horizontal volume facing the street is intended to reflect the scale of neighboring structures, while the narrow two-story volumes are perpendicular to the street, reducing their apparent scale.

This house is designed in strong counterpoint to many of the houses built in the last era of abundant resources, expensive materials, and limitless floor area. The house is not large; it comprises three bedrooms and 2400 square feet (223 square meters). The house is constructed with modest materials that include concrete floors throughout the first floor, oak flooring on the second floor, and plastic laminate and oak millwork.

The house was designed to achieve a balance between recognition of the picturesque Chesapeake Bay landscape, and a more intimate, secluded garden environment. Expansive openings to the private garden combined with smaller, selectively oriented openings toward the greater landscape allow for a sense of privacy while maintaining a sensibility of direct connection to the rhythms of nature.

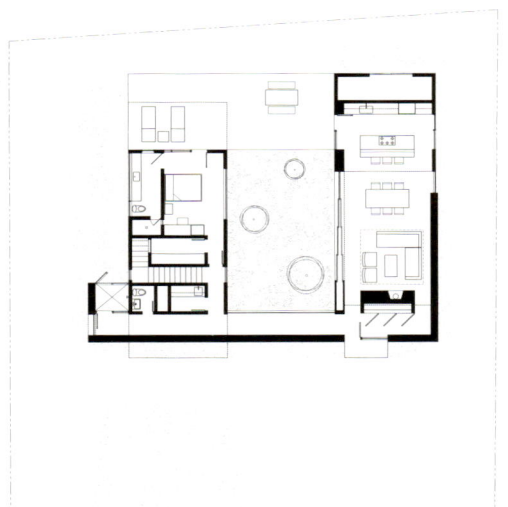

First-floor plan

144

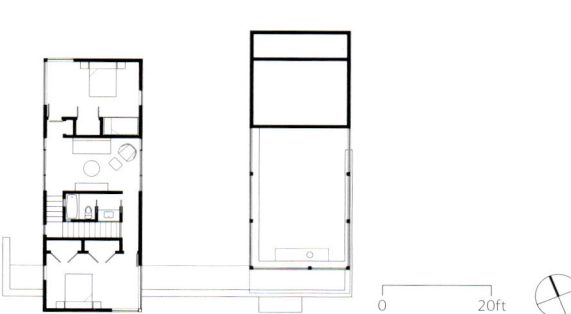

Second-floor plan

LUJAN HOUSE

LUJAN HOUSE 149

LYON PARK HOUSE
Arlington, Virginia

Lyon Park, in Arlington, Virginia is an "urban village" near Washington, D.C. Most of the houses in this established neighborhood were constructed in the 1920s and 1930s. The houses vary in style, ranging from small single-story bungalows to larger wood and brick Colonial Revivalist houses. Streets are tree-lined and the topography is gently rolling. After living in their house for about seven years, a young family of four hoped to transform their Colonial house to better fit their lifestyle. A series of small but cozy rooms failed to connect with each other and to the deep, sloping landscaped backyard. Excluding the basement, the existing house comprised less than 1400 square feet (13 square meters), with two bedrooms and only one full bathroom. Ideally, the transformation would retain the "sense of home" while providing spaces open to each other, additional bedrooms, and a better connection to the landscaped site. A building that avoided stylistic mimicry with modern light-filled spaces was desired. Sustainable construction techniques and the use of environmentally sensitive materials were expected.

The budget for this project was moderate. The result is a modest, restrained and compact modern renovation project that respects the scale and rhythm of the street. The project combines three small additions, totaling 250 square feet (23 square meters) with a complete reconfiguration of the existing spaces. The existing second-floor exterior walls and roof were removed and rebuilt to provide spaces on the second floor with high ceilings and light-filled spaces. On the main level, floor-to-ceiling windows allow expansive views to the backyard, while large windows on the street side ensure a connection to the neighborhood. The previously dark and compartmentalized house is now open and flooded with light.

The FSC-certified wood siding, combined with gray stucco and charcoal fiber cement panels provide a quiet, warm exterior that recedes into the tree-lined streetscape. The compact massing with simple fenestration is organized to respect the scale of adjacent houses. A rain screen system is employed to provide a ventilated envelope. Windows with high-level efficiency ratings provide transparency and light transmission without compromising the performance of the envelope.

Ultimately this is a modest project with a moderate budget. Although this project is very small on many levels, the impact on the lives of this family of four is substantial.

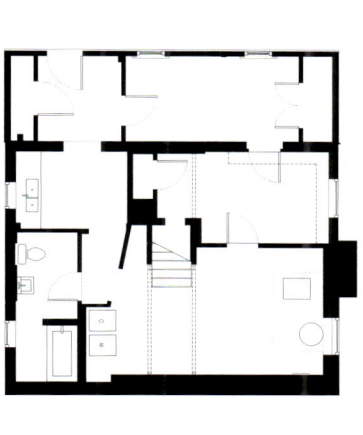

Ground-floor plan (before)

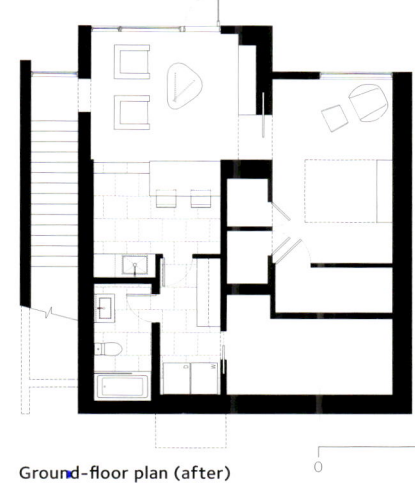

Ground-floor plan (after)

LYON PARK HOUSE

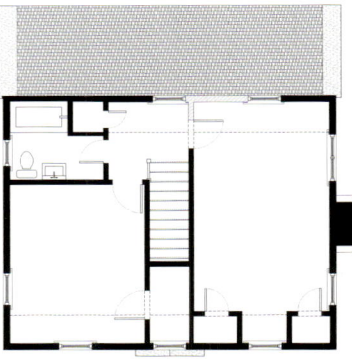

Second-floor plan (before)

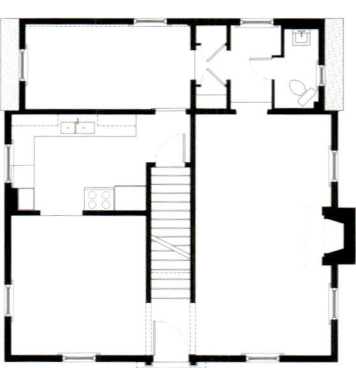

First-floor plan (before)

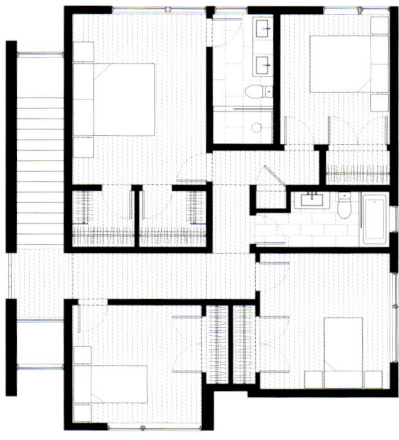

Second-floor plan (after)

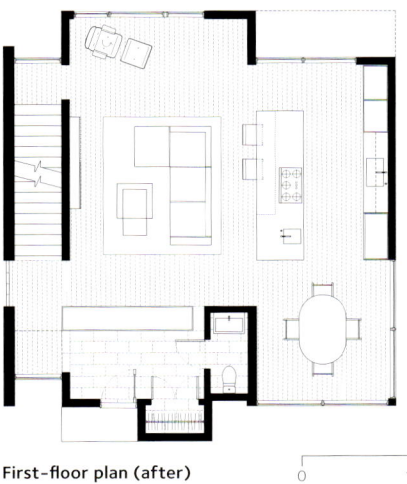

First-floor plan (after)

0   10ft

MOHICAN HILLS HOUSE

Glen Echo, Maryland

Mohican Hills is a small community in Glen Echo, Maryland, within very close proximity to Washington, D.C. This community boasts an unusually high percentage of contemporary and mid-century modern houses relative to most Washington, D.C. suburban neighborhoods. This community is adjacent to the Potomac River. Many of the lots have a steep sloping topography and share river views.

This new house in Mohican Hills is located on one such lot. The house is positioned along the ridge of the sloping site and oriented toward distant river views. A linear composition of spaces arranged along the ridge and open to an existing clearing provides a large lawn with minimal site intrusion and preserves the vast majority of mature trees. The house is organized around a two-story living space with an open floor plan that integrates a high-ceilinged volume with intimate spaces adjacent to the double-height space. A small office on the first floor is separated from the living spaces and is convertible to a fifth bedroom. A three-story entry volume separates the master bedroom area from the subsidiary bedrooms.

Expanses of glass provide views into the wooded landscape toward the distant river and animate the house with light. A combination of intersecting spaces ensures light penetration at all times of day and throughout the year.

This house employs a concrete slab throughout the main floor, which provides passive solar energy assistance. The concrete is stained dark with the goal of increasing the potential solar gain and storage. Expanses of Energy Star glass provide an abundance of daylighting while solar-sensitive shades mediate heat gain. Energy efficient appliances, high-efficiency HVAC equipment, wall and ceiling infrastructure with maximum insulation, and a ventilated building envelope are employed with the expectation of reducing fossil fuel consumption. Large operable windows and doors are located to provide natural ventilation and direct access to the outdoors. Thermally modified wood siding is employed as an alternative to exotic or expensive hardwoods. The wood is forest managed and treated, nontoxic, and durable.

MOHICAN HILLS HOUSE

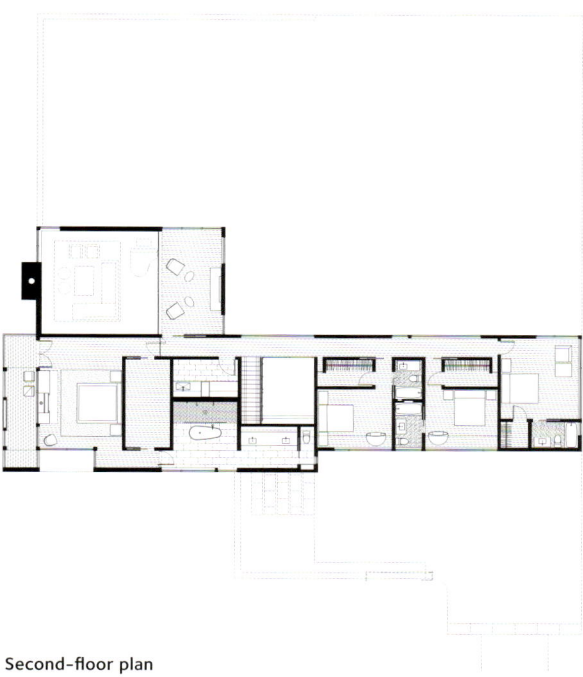

Second-floor plan

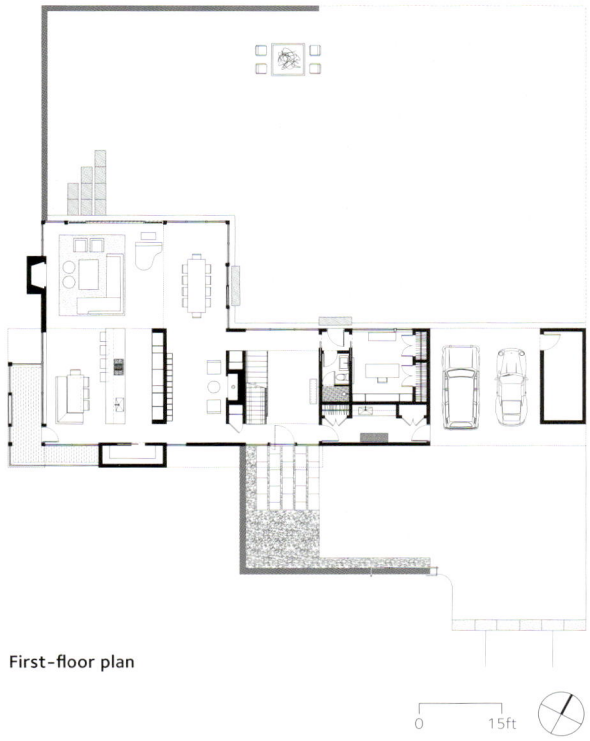

First-floor plan

0 15ft

MOHICAN HILLS HOUSE   169

MOHICAN HILLS HOUSE

MOHICAN HILLS HOUSE

NEVIS POOL AND GARDEN PAVILION

Bethesda, Maryland

Located in a neighborhood bordering Washington, DC, this suburban site has the advantage of being adjacent to woodlands. A contemporary house surrounded by mature trees and manicured gardens anchors the site. A new swimming pool, stone walls, and terraces behind the existing house organize the backyard and establish a dialogue between the existing house and a new pavilion. New paths, trees, and structured plantings reinforce the geometry.

The new pavilion, intended for year-round use, is strategically located to provide a threshold between the structured landscape and adjacent woodland. A low-pitched, terne-coated, stainless-steel roof floats above a dry-stacked slate wall and mahogany volume. Five steel-framed glass doors along with frameless glass walls and mitered glass corners enclose the space, creating an environment that is surrounded by views of the structured landscape, pool, and the adjacent woodland. The doors pivot, so the space can be opened up for much of the year, while a large Rumford fireplace and heated floors provide a cozy counterpoint in winter months.

The interior contains a stainless-steel kitchen with seating, along with a small living space anchored by the fireplace. The bluestone flooring, stone and mahogany walls, and Douglas-fir ceiling create a warm, natural space. This new pavilion is intended to provide shelter from the harsh natural elements, while simultaneously allowing the occupant to enjoy both the beautifully structured garden and the native, natural surroundings.

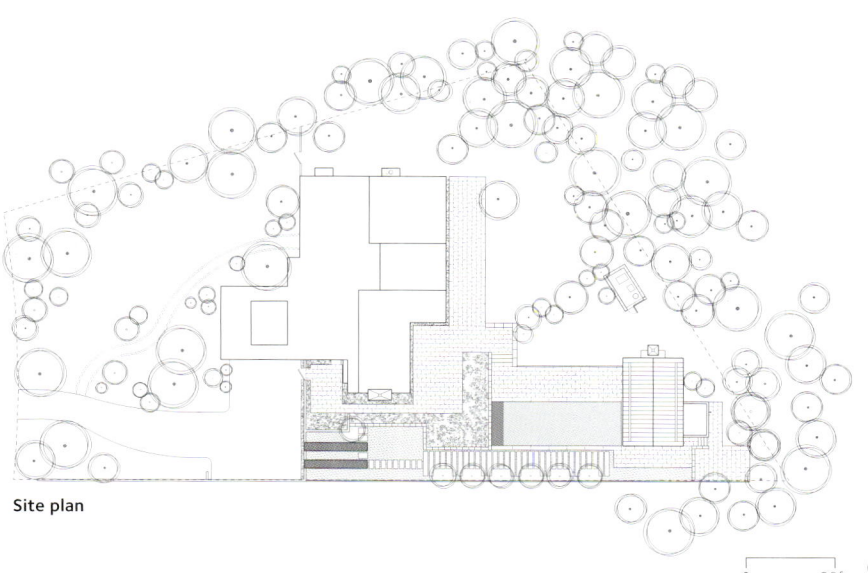

Site plan

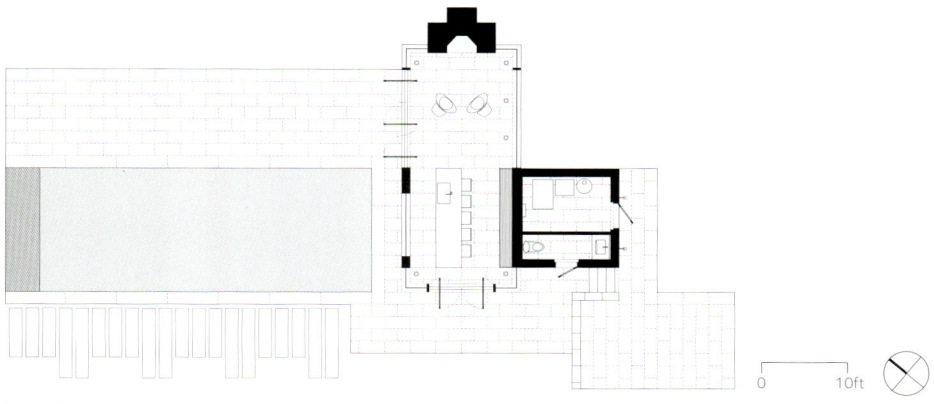

Floor plan

NEVIS POOL AND GARDEN PAVILION 185

OVERLOOK ROAD HOUSE
Washington, D.C.

This project began with a typical post-WWII developer spec house in an established northwest Washington, D.C. neighborhood. Having undergone a series of renovations and additions over time that incorporated varying styles, details, and finishes, the existing house was ultimately composed of disjointed interior spaces. Although the existing spatial arrangement was largely kept intact, the new design integrated expanses of glass, opened up the spaces, and organized them more efficiently. Larger extensions, including a new entry space, a screened porch pavilion, and a second-story office, provided spaces that were requested by the owner, and afforded further opportunities to allow natural light to penetrate the previously dark interiors.

In the redesign, all openings, millwork, and the majority of windows and doors extend from floor to ceiling in order to minimize the impact of the existing 8-foot-high (2.4-meter-high) ceilings. New interior finishes include beech, FSC Rosewood, aluminum, glass, and limestone.

Changes to typical developer houses in desirable neighborhoods are inevitable. While this comprehensive renovation project incorporated significant additional space, the goal was to add a new layer to the existing fabric that respects both the scale and material palette found in the neighborhood.

OVERLOOK ROAD HOUSE

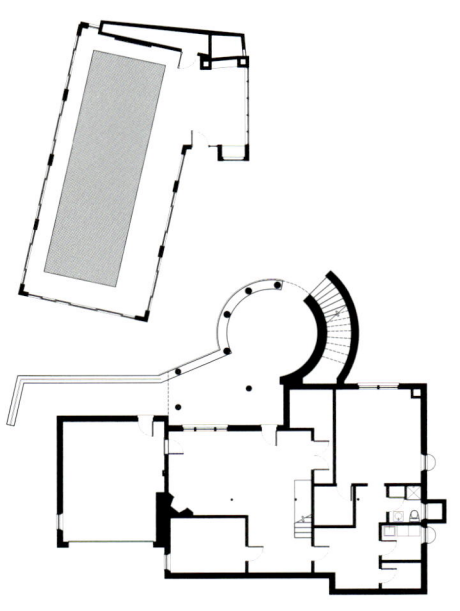
Basement-floor plan (before)

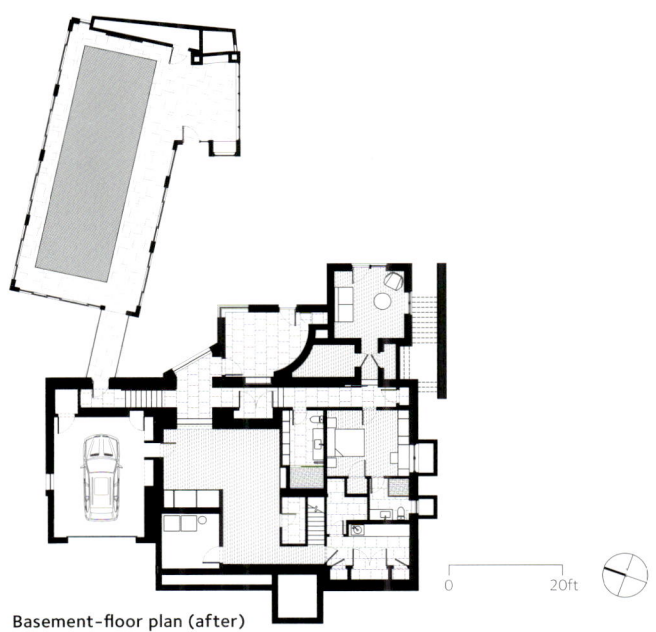
Basement-floor plan (after)

OVERLOOK ROAD HOUSE

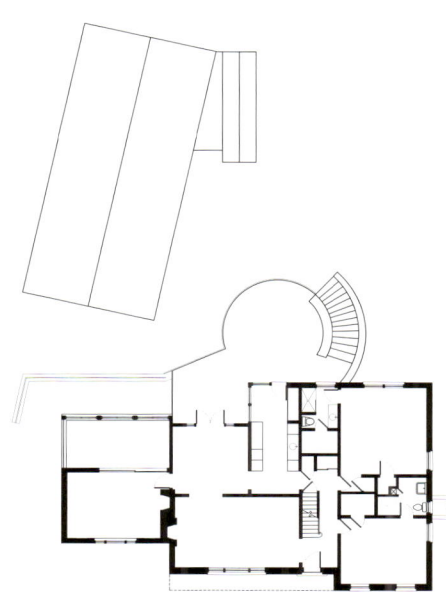

First-floor plan (before)

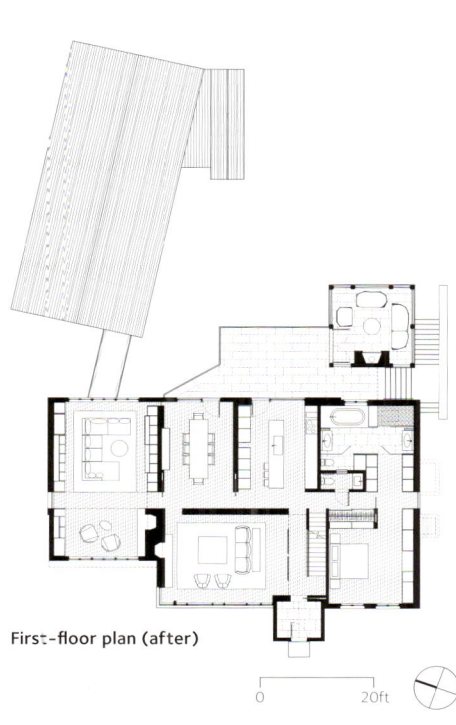

First-floor plan (after)

0   20ft

OVERLOOK ROAD HOUSE   193

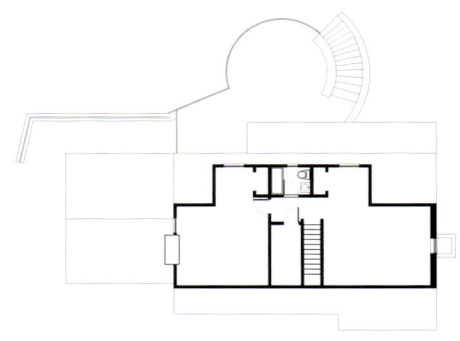

Second-floor plan (before)

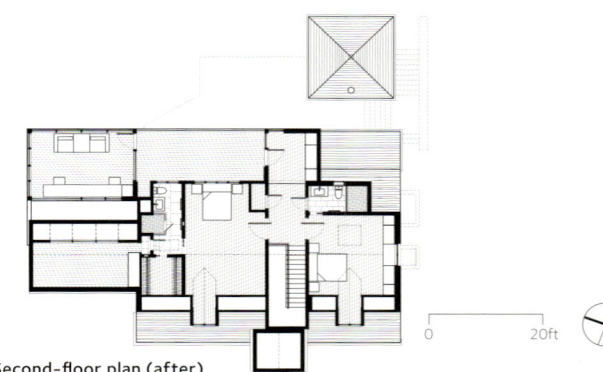

Second-floor plan (after)

RIGGINS HOUSE

Cabin John, Maryland

Located in Cabin John, Maryland, this 4900-square-foot (455-square-meter) house is sited at the end of a manicured lawn, and looks over the edge of a steeply sloping wooded site adjacent to the C&O Canal and the Potomac River. A light-filled, double-height circulation axis separates the house's main volumes, while transverse axes further organize the spaces. Glass and steel bridges cross the circulation space to connect the volumes on the second floor. Primary living spaces bounded by large expanses of glass are oriented towards the river, while secondary spaces open to the lawn.

Large overhangs shield glazing from solar gain in the summer, and provide space for outdoor living, even in inclement weather. With geothermal HVAC, natural lighting, and operable windows and doors to provide cross ventilation, the house remains energy efficient despite employing a large amount of glass.

Interiors are minimally detailed. Finishes include honed and chiseled Pompeii stone, ash flooring, walnut millwork, and white marble countertops. The interior is designed to allow views toward the woods and river to provide the primary visual experience.

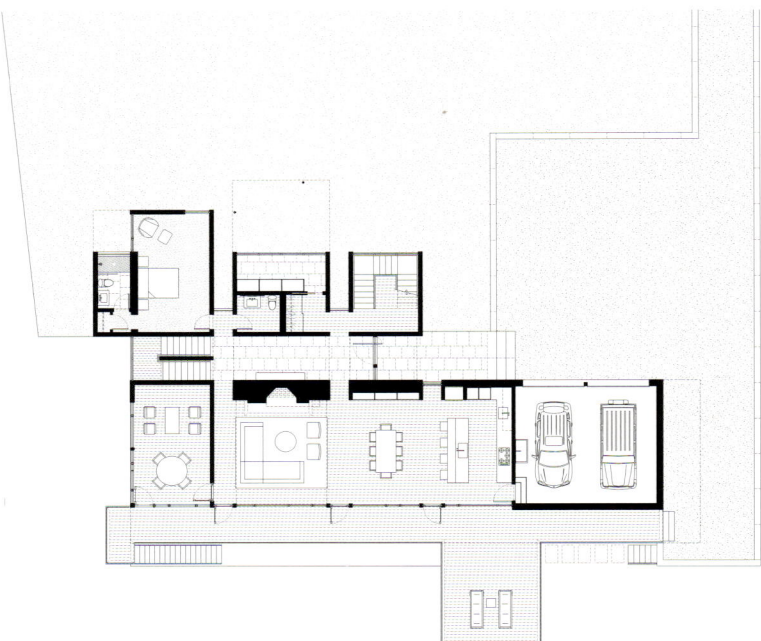

First-floor plan

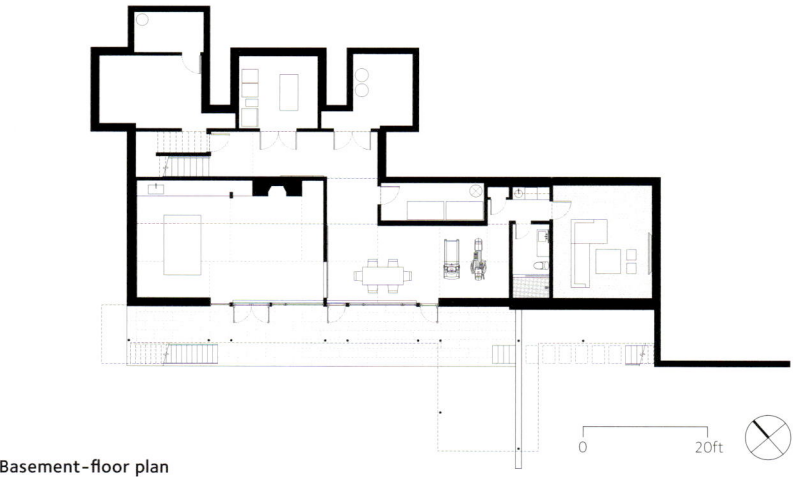

Basement-floor plan

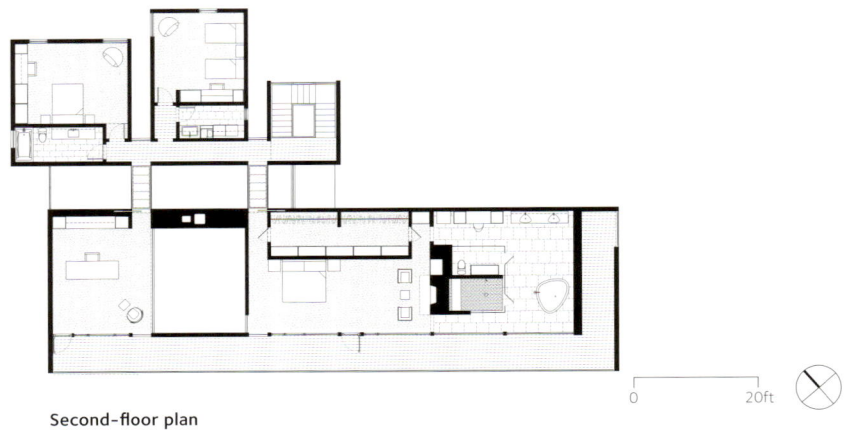

Second-floor plan

RIGGINS HOUSE 209

RIGGINS HOUSE

SEA DEL HOUSE

Bethany Beach, Delaware

Sea Del Estates is small, gated oceanfront community located in Bethany Beach, Delaware. The majority of the 42 houses located in the community are second homes used primarily during the summer months. Most of the houses were originally constructed in the 1970s and 1980s and are simple wood-framed structures. To protect against potential flooding, County ordinances require that the houses be elevated 12 feet (3.7 meters) above sea level. Consequently, these houses were typically framed on wood piles. Building codes also require that enclosed space located below the mean flood level be constructed with "break-away" walls. These walls will come apart in the event of a major storm and subsequent flooding.

The starting point for this project was a small wood-framed structure located on an oceanfront lot. The existing house was less than optimal in terms of size, layout, and openness to the ocean views. Years of exposure to the ocean winds, blowing sand and salt water, had taken its toll physically on the structure as well. Updated Delaware Natural Resource and Environmental Control (DNREC) guidelines are very restrictive and require a new house to be built much farther from the ocean than where the current oceanfront houses are built. The DNREC guidelines allow you to rebuild on existing piles, but you cannot build new pilings on the ocean side of the newly established "DNREC Line". These requirements would ultimately influence the design of this project.

The new house and oceanfront decks are designed above 22 pre-existing wood piles located within the prescribed DNREC area. Eight newly constructed piles, located outside the DNREC area allow for expansion of the building envelope. The layout of the existing pilings significantly informed many of the design decisions and affected all structural components. The new house is composed of three volumes, which incorporate all living spaces, an elevator tower, a large oceanfront deck and a second small side deck, where one had previously been located. Exterior materials, including fiber cement panels and integrally colored cement stucco are chosen for their durability and relative low maintenance. Wood slats are employed on the south side of the house and on most of the lower level away from the ocean, allowing breezes to pass through. These slats are also incorporated on the west wall of the new stairwell to allow light to filter into the space while minimizing the amount of harsh western sunlight penetrating into the interior.

In the new living, dining and kitchen spaces, floor-to-ceiling panels of glass slide completely open to the new deck, providing a contiguous indoor / outdoor environment with ocean views. Similarly sized, sliding screen panels operate to provide a

"screened porch" allowing continued outdoor living while being protected from the elements.

This new house is designed to hover above the adjacent dunes while providing expansive views toward the Atlantic Ocean. Interior finishes are limited to walnut flooring and white-painted millwork. The palette is intentionally simple and minimal. Detailing is crisp. The views and interaction with the outdoors are intended to provide the primary sensory experiences.

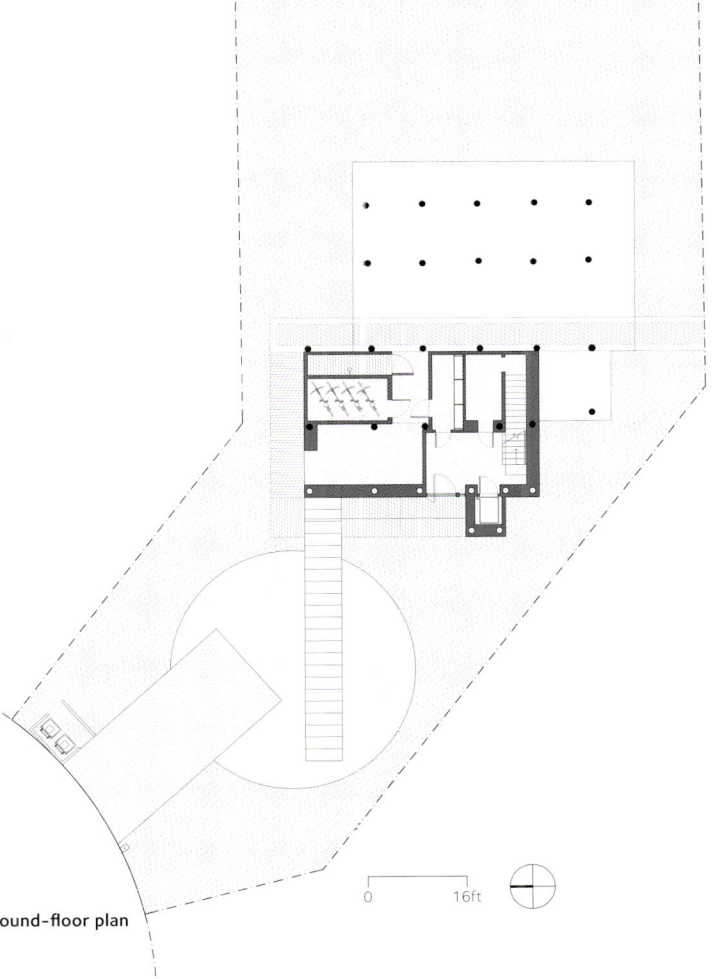

Ground-floor plan

SEA DEL HOUSE

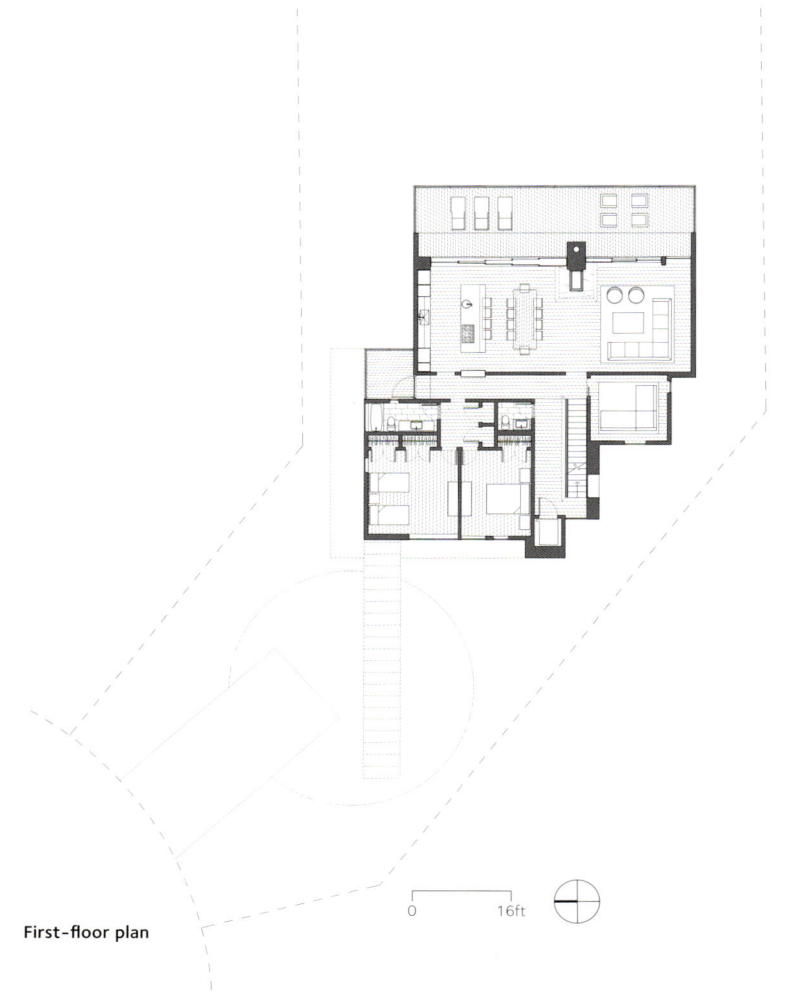

First-floor plan

0 16ft

SEA DEL HOUSE

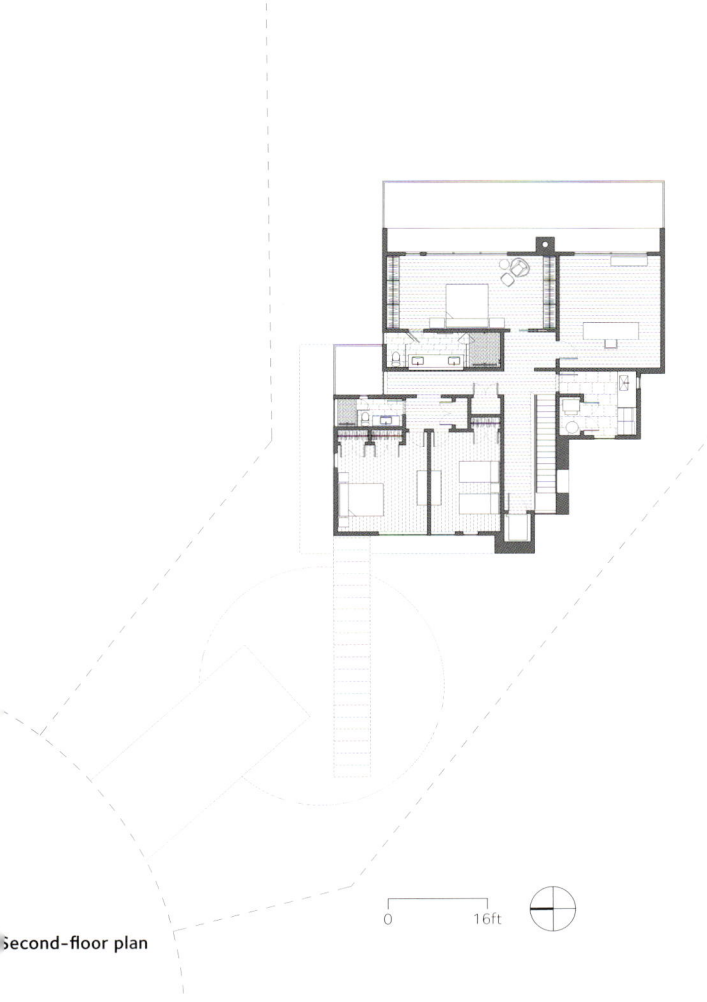

Second-floor plan

0   16ft

SEA DEL HOUSE   225

SEA DEL HOUSE

SHARMA MATHUR HOUSE

Washington, D.C.

A young couple, with a growing family were gradually feeling squeezed for space in their recently constructed, modern, upscale Washington, D.C. condominium. The couple hoped to find a larger space, but with similar light-filled qualities and an open floor plan. They also desired to stay in their current West End neighborhood. The couple extended their search to include nearby single-family houses, because they were unable to find a larger version of the loft-like space. Ultimately, the search led to an unrenovated, three-story row house, located a few blocks from their existing building. The couple viewed this as an opportunity to transform the house to accommodate their spatial needs, open floor plan and desired finish materials.

The existing house comprised dark, cramped and compartmentalized spaces. The kitchen was isolated in the rear corner of the house. Period detailing, massive fireplaces and a large, heavy staircase were in contrast to the couple's desire for open, clean-lined and light-filled spaces.

The house was gutted and reorganized to best achieve the clients' project goals. This allowed for new infrastructure, a super-insulated building envelope, energy-efficient HVAC and electrical systems, and new finishes. The kitchen is relocated to the center of the house and is open to the living and dining spaces. The kitchen island is shaped to modulate work and seating areas. This geometry is intended to provide a counterpoint to the orthogonal lines defined by the inherited rectangular footprint of the building. Interior, angled walls placed in an existing projecting bay reinforce this geometry. An open-riser staircase and large skylight infuse the three floors with light. Built-in furniture and millwork provide ample storage and help minimize clutter. Bright orange panels that conceal a powder room and large closet offset a predominantly muted color palette.

Two children's bedrooms with a shared bathroom and a generous master bedroom suite occupy the second floor. The third floor is reserved for a guest bedroom and family / playroom designed to open to a future rooftop deck.

The design provides this young family with a new, light-filled house, organized to fulfill spatial needs and comprises open, clean-lined and simply detailed spaces.

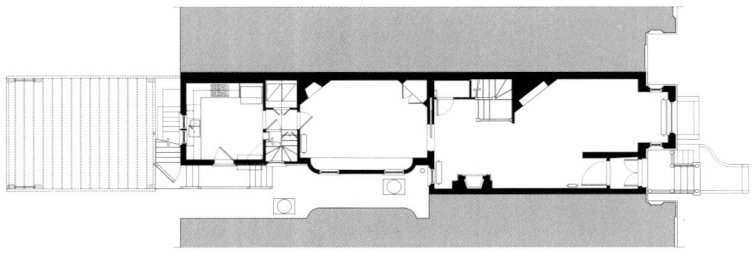

First-floor plan (before)

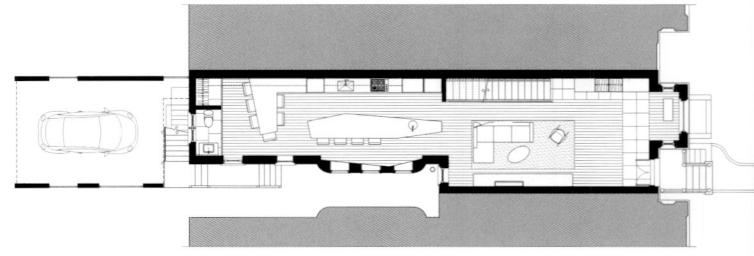

First-floor plan (after)

SHARMA MATHUR HOUSE

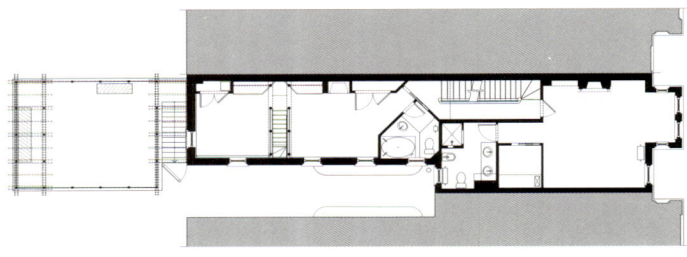
Second-floor plan (before)

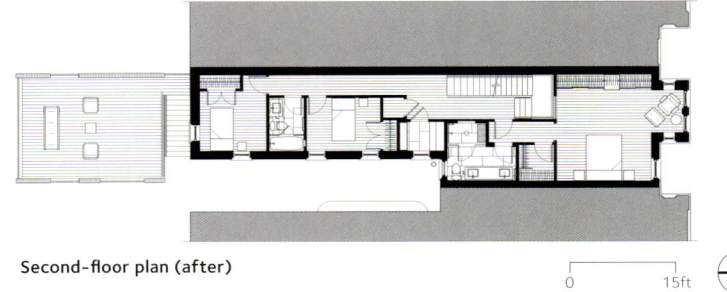
Second-floor plan (after)

0   15ft

232

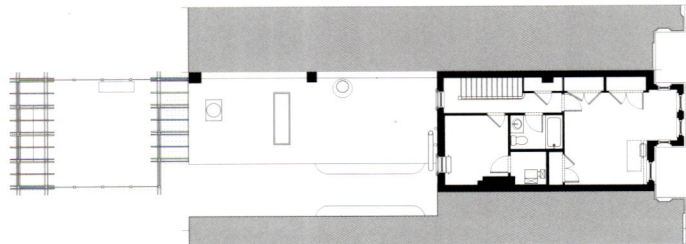
Third-floor plan (before)

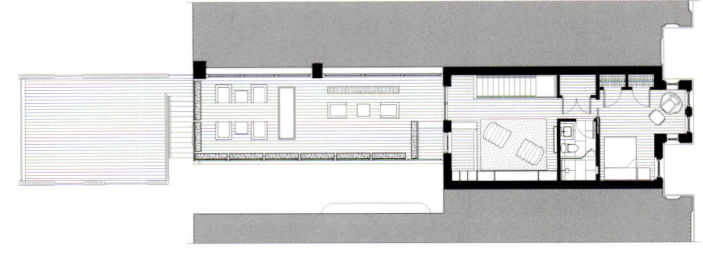
Third-floor plan (after)

0 15ft

SHARMA MATHUR HOUSE

TRED AVON RIVER HOUSE

Easton, Maryland

Easton, Maryland is located in Talbot County on Maryland's eastern shore, and was established in 1710. Easton remains largely agrarian, with numerous farms interspersed among the area's many waterways.

Diverging from several acres of cornfields, a quarter-mile (402-meter) road, lined with pine trees, terminates at a diamond-shaped tract of land, with breathtaking views of the Tred Avon River. Arising from the gravel drive and hedge-lined parking court, this new house is unveiled as three solid volumes, linked together with glass bridges that are suspended above the landscape. The central 36-foot-high (11-meter-high) volume is mostly devoid of fenestration, punctuated only by the recessed 10-foot-high (3-meter-high) entry door, and narrow sidelights. The contrasting 12-foot-high (3.7-meter-high) western volume contains a garage and additional service space, while the eastern volume, floating above grade, contains the primary living spaces.

After entering the house and passing through one of the glass bridges, the transformation begins. Initially presented as solid and austere, the house unfolds into a 124-foot-long (37.8-meter-long) living volume, light-filled and wrapped in glass with panoramic views of the river. A grid of steel columns modulates the space. Covered terraces extend the interior spaces, providing an abundance of outdoor living space with varying exposures and views. A screened porch, located on an axis to the main seating group, provides an additional forum to experience views of the river, as it overlooks a swimming pool.

A geothermal mechanical system, solar tubes, hydronic floor heating, and a concrete floor slab provide thermal mass, and large overhangs above the terraces prevent heat gain, and minimize dependence on fossil fuels. The entire house is elevated 4 feet (1.2 meters) above grade to protect against anticipated flooding.

The house is crisply detailed and minimally furnished to allow views of the picturesque site to provide the primary sensory experience. The house was designed as a vehicle to experience and enjoy the incredibly beautiful landscape, known as Diamond Point, seamlessly blending the river's expansive vista with the space.

TRED AVON RIVER HOUSE

TRED AVON RIVER HOUSE

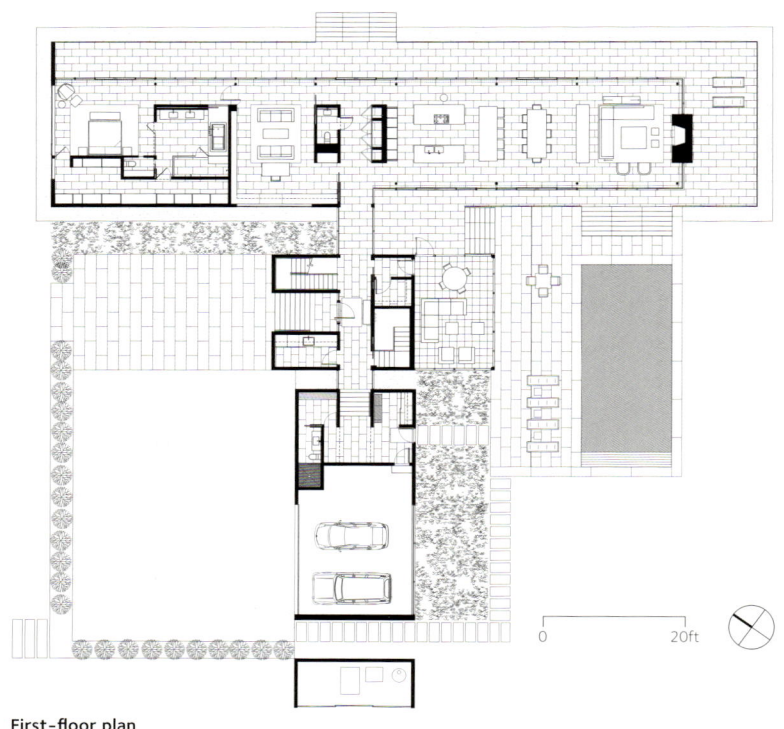

First-floor plan

TRED AVON RIVER HOUSE

TRED AVON RIVER HOUSE

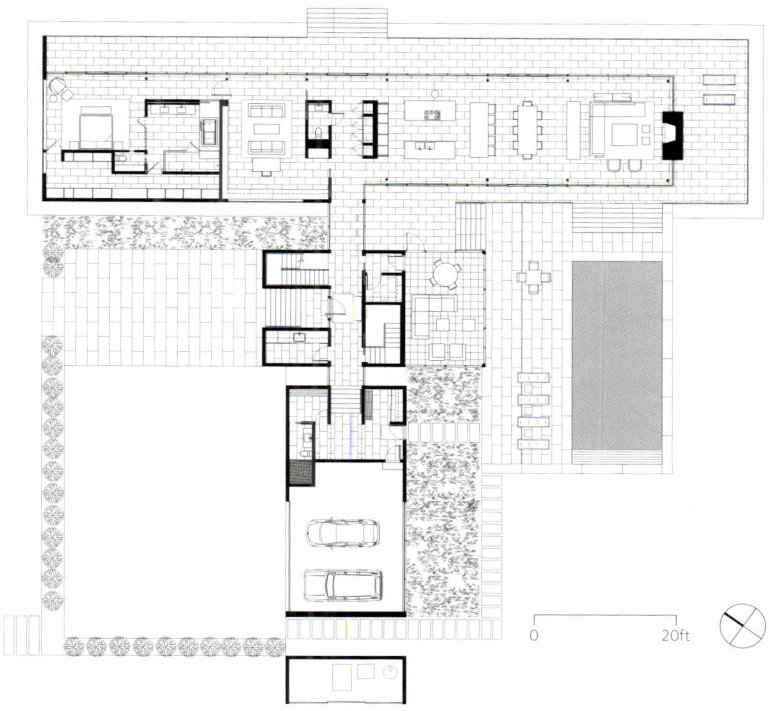

Second-floor plan

TRED AVON RIVER HOUSE

TWINING ROAD HOUSE RENOVATION

Potomac, Maryland

After living in their house for more than 30 years, this 'empty nest' couple decided it was time to 'freshen up' their 1980s ranch-style dwelling. The owners did not have preconceived ideas or specific programmatic goals, but instead were open minded, and requested design solutions potentially varying in scope.

The owners originally built this house, located in Potomac, Maryland, to accommodate their young family. The house underwent a series of renovations and additions over 30 years, adjusting to varying needs and changing family dynamics. Although these alterations served the family well, the numerous changes were not stylistically coherent or consistent in their architectural details. The generally dark, existing house retained a compartmentalized kitchen and failed to take advantage of views toward the wooded parkland just beyond the property.

This most recent renovation attempts to improve the organization of the house, and provide a more open floor plan, infuse the house with natural light, and focus views toward the woodlands. The desire was to create a new scheme that was updated, comprehensive and unified, while adding minimal square footage. The additional space allows a home office to be relocated from the basement. With high ceilings and an abundance of glass, this space is oriented to take advantage of the wooded views. The kitchen is reoriented, enlarged, and opens up to a dining space, living room and views of the landscape. The master bedroom and bathroom are repositioned to maximize orientation toward the views, and reorganized to facilitate daily routines. Interior finishes, including wenge flooring and rift-sawn oak millwork, are intended to unify and enrich the interior spaces. Detailing is minimal and crisp, allowing natural light and views to take center stage.

With their strong emotional ties and an affinity for the house developed over so many years, the redesign became a balancing act between retaining the original house while updating it for the next chapter in this family's life. The redesign allows the original ranch house, with its strong horizontal presence, to anchor a series of vertical volumes that enrich the house with light and optimal views to the landscape beyond.

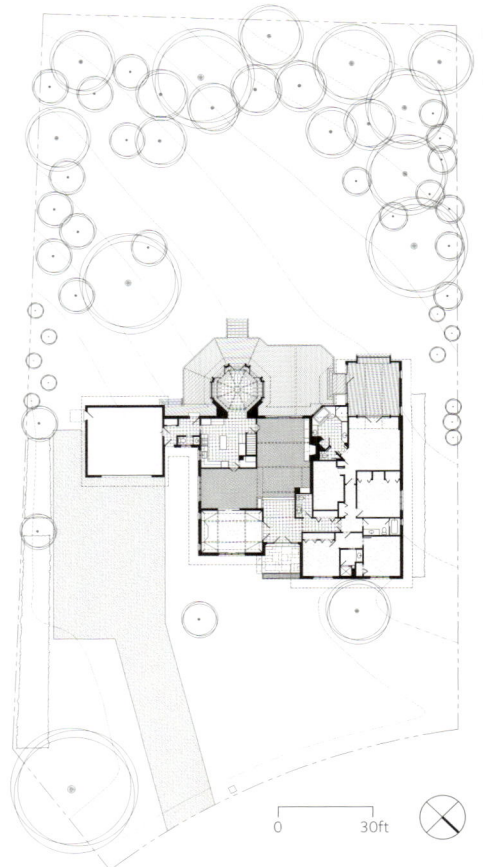

Ground-floor plan (before)

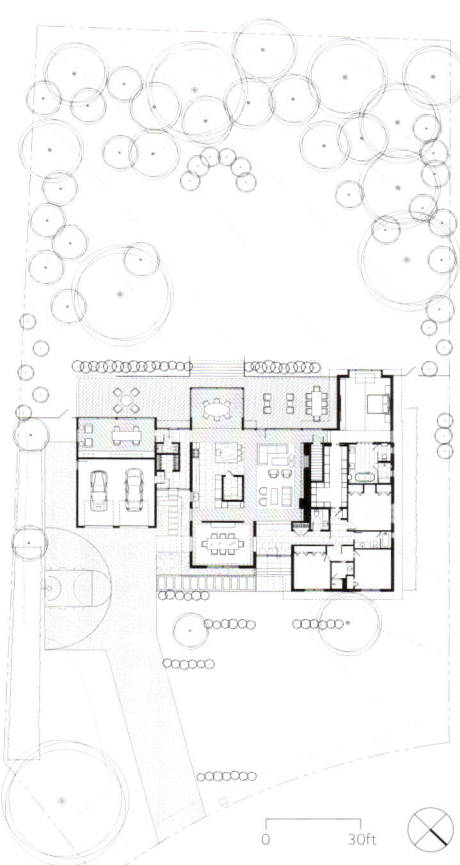

Ground-floor plan (after)

TWINING ROAD HOUSE RENOVATION   261

TWINING ROAD HOUSE RENOVATION

WATERGATE APARTMENT
Washington, D.C.

The Watergate complex in Washington, D.C. consists of five buildings sited on 10 acres (4 hectares) overlooking the Potomac River, and was built between 1963 and 1972. Designed by Italian Architect Luigi Moretti, the Watergate is considered one of Washington's most desirable addresses.

This 1250-square-foot (116-square-meter) unit is located on the 14th floor and had never been renovated. Compartmentalized spaces, with ceiling heights less than 8 feet 4 inches (1.4 meters) high, presented the perception of a low, horizontal environment. Offsetting these less than optimal existing conditions are spectacular views along the Potomac River looking toward the landmark Francis Scott Key Bridge.

The interior was gutted to the essential structure, and plumbing, electrical, and mechanical infrastructure. Flooring was removed to the concrete slab. In reference to the client's program and in deference to the view, the space was reconfigured with a formal clarity to provide open living spaces with river-view orientation. An integral plastered wall initiated near the entry organizes the apartment and angles to direct views along the river and toward the Key Bridge. Planar walls and cabinetry elements combine with clear and translucent glass to further organize and define spaces.

An extended material palette is intended to be subtle and refined. Detailing is minimal and crisp. White terrazzo flooring becomes the stage for walnut wall paneling, white ash millwork, luminous glass walls, integral charcoal plaster, aluminum, and black concrete. Strips of stainless steel are inset into the white terrazzo to reinforce established geometries and floating ceiling planes. Forms and textures serve to both unify and diversify spatial qualities.

In this project the architecture is intended to provide a framework for the furnishings and the view, while minimizing the sense of the pre-existing low, horizontal environment.

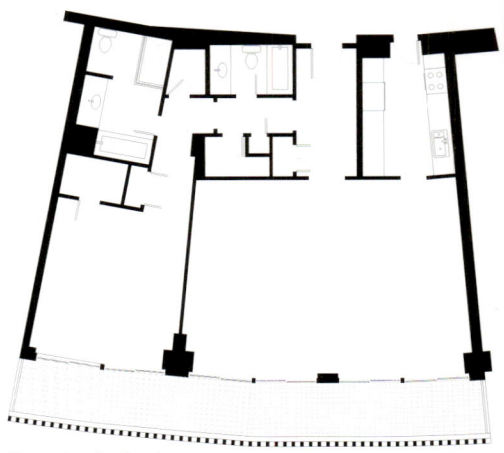

Floor plan (before)

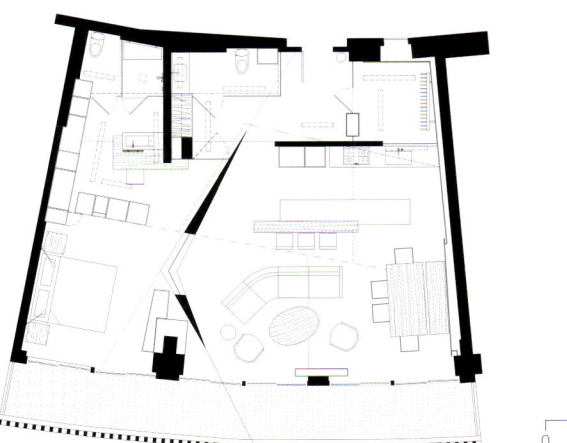

Floor plan (after)

0 8ft

WATERGATE APARTMENT

WATERGATE APARTMENT

WISSIOMING2

Bethesda, Maryland

Located in Glen Echo, Maryland, just outside of Washington, D.C., this new house is sited on a sloping, wooded lot with distant views of the Potomac River. The house is positioned to preserve a majority of mature trees and is oriented toward the river views and south-facing slope. The house is organized into two volumes, which are separated by a reflecting pool. Glass bridges span the pool, connecting the two volumes. Secondary volumes intersect and overlap the two larger structures, rendering the composition more dynamic. Material changes in the various elements intensify the relationships. Expanses of glass open to a terrace that is organized around a swimming pool with two "infinity" edges, reinforcing the connectivity to the wooded landscape.

The interiors are painted with light. Walls constructed with slender steel window frames, composed in "'Mondrian"-inspired patterns, combine with translucent panels, wenge and white oak millwork, and Pompeii Scarpaletto stone to define interior spaces. White terrazzo flooring contrasts against the black window frames and unifies the volumes on the main floor.

This house is designed such that the architecture becomes subservient to the landscape that surrounds it, providing spaces that are organized to integrate an inherently picturesque site.

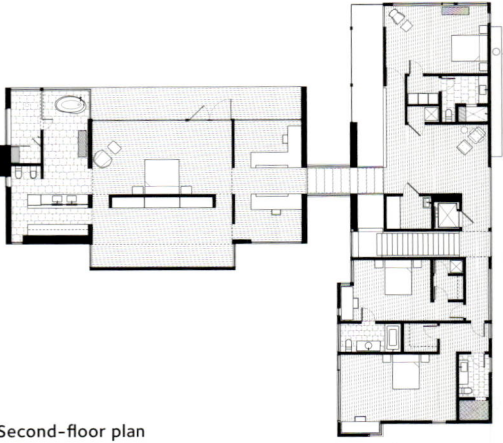

Second-floor plan

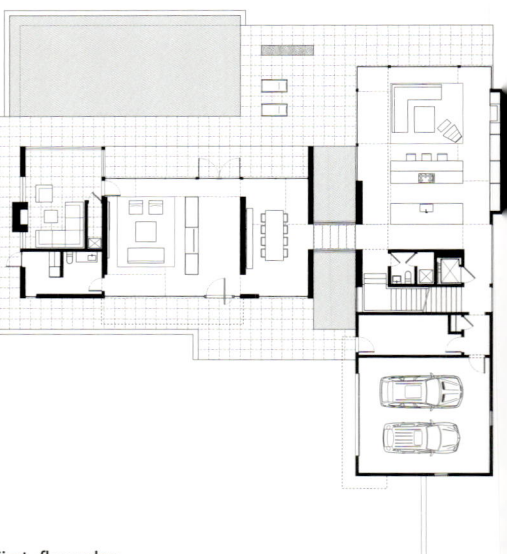

First-floor plan

CREDITS

ARCHITECT

Robert M. Gurney, FAIA, Architect
5110 1/2 MacArthur Boulevard NW
Washington, D.C. 20016, United States
t (202) 237-0925 / **f** (202) 237-0927
e rmg@robertgurneyarchitect.com

PROJECT CONTRIBUTORS

4 SPRINGS LANE Page 12
Rappahannock County, Virginia, United States
Date of completion: 2013

Project Architect
Brian Tuskey
Interior Designer
Therese Baron Gurney, ASID
Baron Gurney Interiors
Landscape Architect
Kevin Campion
Campion Hruby Landscape Architects
Structural Engineer
D. Anthony Beale LLC
Contractor
Erwin Opitz
Opitz Construction Consulting, Inc.
Photographer
Maxwell MacKenzie Architectural Photographer

308 MULBERRY STREET Page 24
Lewes, Delaware, United States
Date of completion: 2011

Project Architect
Brian Tuskey
Interior Designer
Therese Baron Gurney, ASID
Baron Gurney Interiors
Landscape Architect
South Fork Studio, Landscape Architecture
Structural Engineer
D. Anthony Beale LLC
Contractor
Ilex Construction
Photographer
Maxwell MacKenzie Architectural Photographer

APARTMENT 24 Page 38
Washington, D.C., United States
Date of completion: 2012

>**Project Architect**
>Kara R. McHone
>**Interior Designer**
>Therese Baron Gurney, ASID
>Baron Gurney Interiors
>**Contractor**
>Added Dimensions, Inc.
>**Photographer**
>Maxwell MacKenzie Architectural Photographer

BECHERER HOUSE Page 48
Earlysville, Virginia, United States
Date of completion: 2011

>**Project Architect**
>Claire L. Andreas
>**Interior Designer**
>Therese Baron Gurney, ASID
>Baron Gurney Interiors
>**Landscape Architect**
>Kevin Campion
>Campion Hruby Landscape Architects
>**Structural Engineer**
>D. Anthony Beale LLC
>**Contractor**
>Bruce Gordon
>Shelter Associates, Ltd
>**Photographer**
>Maxwell MacKenzie Architectural Photographer

BM MODULAR ONE Page 60
Bethesda, Maryland, United States
Date of completion: 2013

>**Project Architect**
>Kara R. McHone
>**Interior Designer**
>Therese Baron Gurney, ASID
>Baron Gurney Interiors
>**Landscape Architect**
>Kevin Campion
>Campion Hruby Landscape Architects
>**Structural Engineer**
>D. Anthony Beale LLC
>**General Contractor**
>Sandy Spring Builders
>**Pre-fab Contractor**
>Nationwide Homes
>**Photographer**
>Maxwell MacKenzie Architectural Photographer

BRANDYWINE HOUSE Page 72
Washington, D.C., United States
Date of completion: 2013

Project Architect
Claire L. Andreas
Landscape Architect
Kevin Campion
Campion Hruby Landscape Architects
Structural Engineer
D. Anthony Beale LLC
Contractor
Sandy Spring Builders
Photographer
Anice Hoachlander and Allen Russ
Hoachlander Davis Photography

DIFFICULT RUN RESIDENCE Page 84
McLean, Virginia, United States
Date of completion: 2012

Project Architect
John Riordan
Landscape Architect
Lila Fendrick Landscape Architects
Structural Engineer
D. Anthony Beale LLC
Contractor
Phase 1
Peterson & Collins
Phase 2
Commonwealth Building and Design
Photographer
Maxwell MacKenzie Architectural Photographer

HAMPDEN LANE HOUSE Page 96
Bethesda, Maryland, United States
Date of completion: 2010

Project Architect
Brian Tuskey
Structural Engineer
D. Anthony Beale LLC
Contractor
Freedom First Homes
Photographer
Maxwell MacKenzie Architectural Photographer

HOUSE ON SOLITUDE CREEK Page 106
St. Michaels, Maryland, United States
Date of completion: 2015

> **Project Architect**
> Kara McHone
> **Structural Engineer**
> D. Anthony Beale LLC
> **Contractor**
> Thinkmakebuild
> **Photographer**
> Anice Hoachlander
> Hoachlander Davis Photography

KOMAI RESIDENCE Page 118
Alexandria, Virginia, United States
Date of completion: 2013

> **Project Architect**
> Brian Tuskey
> **Structural Engineer**
> D. Anthony Beale LLC
> **Contractor**
> Commonwealth Building and Design
> **Photographer**
> Maxwell MacKenzie Architectural Photographer

LORBER TARLER RESIDENCE Page 130
Washington, D.C., United States
Date of completion: 2009

> **Project Architect**
> Brian Tuskey
> **Interior Designer**
> Therese Baron Gurney, ASID
> Baron Gurney Interiors
> **Structural Engineer**
> D. Anthony Beale LLC
> **Contractor**
> Prill Construction
> **Photographer**
> Paul Warchol
> Paul Warchol Photography

LUJAN HOUSE Page 140

Ocean View, Delaware, United States
Date of completion: 2009

Project Architect
Claire L. Andreas
Interior Designer
Therese Baron Gurney, ASID
Baron Gurney Interiors
Structural Engineer
D. Anthony Beale LLC
Contractor
Gude and Conard, Inc.
Photographer
Anice Hoachlander
Hoachlander Davis Photography

LYON PARK HOUSE Page 152

Arlington, Virginia, United States
Date of completion: 2015

Project Architect
Claire L. Andreas
Structural Engineer
D. Anthony Beale LLC
Contractor
Arta Construction
Photographer
Anice Hoachlander
Hoachlander Davis Photography

MOHICAN HILLS HOUSE Page 164

Glen Echo, Maryland, United States
Date of completion: 2015

Project Architect
Sarah A. Mailhot
Landscape Architect
Kevin Campion
Campion Hruby Landscape Architects
Structural Engineer
D. Anthony Beale LLC
Contractor
Commonwealth Building and Design
Photographer
Anice Hoachlander
Hoachlander Davis Photography

NEVIS POOL AND GARDEN PAVILION Page 178

Bethesda, Maryland, United States

Date of completion: 2011

Project Architect
John Riordan
Structural Engineer
D. Anthony Beale LLC
Contractor
Peterson & Collins
Photographer
Maxwell MacKenzie Architectural Photographer

OVERLOOK ROAD HOUSE Page 186

Washington, D.C., United States

Date of completion: 2013

Project Architect
John Riordan
Interior Designer
Therese Baron Gurney, ASID
Baron Gurney Interiors
Landscape Architect
Kevin Campion
Campion Hruby Landscape Architects
Structural Engineer
D. Anthony Beale LLC
Contractor
Added Dimensions, Inc.
Photographer
Anice Hoachlander
Hoachlander Davis Photography

RIGGINS HOUSE Page 200

Cabin John, Maryland, United States

Date of completion: 2013

Project Architect
Brian Tuskey
Interior Designer
Therese Baron Gurney, ASID
Baron Gurney Interiors
Structural Engineer
D. Anthony Beale LLC
Contractor
Sandy Spring Builders
Photographer
Maxwell MacKenzie Architectural Photographer

SEA DEL HOUSE Page 214
Bethany Beach, Delaware, United States
Date of completion: 2015

    Project Architect
    Sarah A. Mailhot
    Structural Engineer
    Long, Tann & D'Onofrio Structural Engineers
    Contractor
    Bruce Mears
    Photographer
    Anice Hoachlander
    Hoachlander Davis Photography

SHARMA MATHUR HOUSE Page 228
Washington, D.C., United States
Date of completion: 2015

    Project Architect
    Sarah A. Mailhot
    Interior Designer
    Therese Baron Gurney, ASID
    Baron Gurney Interiors
    Structural Engineer
    D. Anthony Beale LLC
    Contractor
    MCA Remodeling
    Photographer
    Anice Hoachlander
    Hoachlander Davis Photography

TRED AVON RIVER HOUSE Page 240
Easton, Maryland, United States
Date of completion: 2012

    Project Architect
    Brian Tuskey
    Interior Designer
    Therese Baron Gurney, ASID
    Baron Gurney Interiors
    Landscape Architect
    Lila Fendrick Landscape Architects
    Structural Engineer
    D. Anthony Beale LLC
    Contractor
    Peterson & Collins
    Photographer
    Maxwell MacKenzie Architectural Photographer

TWINING ROAD HOUSE RENOVATION Page 256

Potomac, Maryland, United States

Date of completion: 2014

Project Architects
Claire L. Andreas

Kara R. McHone

Interior Designer
Therese Baron Gurney, ASID

Baron Gurney Interiors

Landscape Architect
Kevin Campion

Campion Hruby Landscape Architects

Structural Engineer
D. Anthony Beale LLC

Contractor
Added Dimensions, Inc.

Photographer
Anice Hoachlander

Hoachlander Davis Photography

WATERGATE APARTMENT Page 270

Washington, D.C., United States

Date of completion: 2010

Project Architect
Sarah A. Mailhot

Interior Designer
Therese Baron Gurney, ASID

Baron Gurney Interiors

Contractor
Added Dimensions, Inc.

Photographer
Maxwell MacKenzie Architectural Photographer

WISSIOMING2 Page 282

Bethesda, Maryland

Date of completion: 2011

Project Architect
Brian Tuskey

Structural Engineer
D. Anthony Beale LLC

Contractor
Bloom Builders

Photographer
Maxwell MacKenzie Architectural Photographer

Every effort has been made to trace the original source of copyright material contained in this book. The publishers would be pleased to hear from copyright holders to rectify any errors or omissions.

The information and illustrations in this publication have been prepared and supplied by Robert M. Gurney and the contributors. While all reasonable efforts have been made to ensure accuracy, the publishers do not, under any circumstances, accept responsibility for errors, omissions and representations express or implied.